Brushing up on Believing

Brushing up on Believing

A fresh look at
basic Christianity and prayer

Shelagh Brown and Gavin Reid

Illustrations by Taffy

 the bible reading fellowship

The Bible Reading Fellowship
Warwick House
25 Buckingham Palace Road
London SW1W OPP

First published 1991

British Library Cataloguing in Publication Data

Reid, Gavin
Brushing up on believing: a fresh look at basic
Christianity and prayer.
1. Christian life. Faith
I. Title   II. Brown, Shelagh   III. Bible Reading Fellowship
248.4

ISBN 0-900164-90-5

Typeset by Cambridge Composing (UK) Ltd
Printed by Bocardo Press Ltd, Didcot, England

Contents

Foreword

by The Rt Revd Dr George Carey

The most urgent task the church has is that of sharing its faith with the world around. Look around at society's disintegrating morality, its ignorance of God, the apathy of many Christians and their failure to relate their faith to life – and you and I will need little convincing that the '90s will be a make-or-break decade.

I have, however, two grounds for my confidence that by the end of this decade the church will be a stronger and larger body.

The first is the power and presence of God. He has not given up believing in the world and in the church, and neither should we. Indeed, his grace and love are daily with us. We can trust in his power to equip his people for the work.

Secondly, we do have resources in the church to inform, challenge and inspire. An example is this splendid volume by Gavin Reid and Shelagh Brown. Written in a popular, light-hearted vein, the book is accessible to a wide variety of people without talking down to any of them.

So it gives me great pleasure to commend *Brushing up on Believing* – I hope it will equip us all to share our faith in attractive ways to the world around.

George Carey

Introduction

We have written this book to go hand in hand with *Lights that Shine* – How Christians can fulfil their call to mission. In our introduction to that book we said that we had wondered whether to have the word 'evangelism' in the title. After all, we were writing it for the Decade of Evangelism. But then we thought that if we asked, 'Would you like to be an evangelist?' some people might be rather alarmed and say, 'No!'

A better question to ask seemed to be, 'Would you like to be lights that shine?' In answer to that we thought most people might smile a little, and say, 'Oh yes!' So we simply called it *Lights that Shine*, because that is what it is about. We have written *Brushing up on Believing* to partner *Lights that Shine*, because the more deeply we believe the more brightly our lights will shine.

We have both worked on both books. I met with Gavin over several months, either in the evenings or on Saturdays, and recorded our discussions on cassette. I word-processed them, wrote the second drafts, and then we worked those over before I produced the final manuscripts. But I have written them in the first person because they read better that way.

We now have considerable sympathy for Archbishop Derek Worlock and Bishop David Sheppard, who do various things together including writing books (one of them, *With Christ in the Wilderness*, for the Bible Reading Fellowship). It may be *Better Together* (the title of one of their previous books) – and we believe it is. But it is also a lot harder!

In this book there are two sections, one on the basic Christian doctrines and the other on the Lord's Prayer. Individuals can simply read straight throught the whole lot on their own, or the two sections can be used as the basis for two courses on brushing up on believing. We have included material at the end of each chapter with questions for discussion, prayers and meditations.

Some readers will be experienced at leading groups, so they may make only a limited use of the material we have provided. But we had in mind the people who are less experienced, or perhaps have never led a group before, and we hope that the way we have set out the material will provide them with all they need.

Some readers will already know Graham Kendrick's song, 'Shine, Jesus, Shine'. Kingsway Publications have given us permission to print the words in both our books, and we are thankful to them for the permission, to Graham Kendrick for writing it, and to the Holy Spirit for inspiring it.

Unusually, because of the importance of the Decade of Evangelism, Kingsway have also given us permission to print the music, and we have done that in *Lights that Shine*. It would be a superb theme song for the Decade. It recognizes that the light of Christ is already shining in the world, but it is a prayer that it will shine even more brightly – both in the world and in our own hearts.

> Lord, the light of Your love is shining
> In the midst of the darkness, shining;
> Jesus, Light of the World, shine upon us,
> Set us free by the truth You now bring us,
> Shine on me, shine on me.
>
> *Chorus* Shine, Jesus, shine,
> Fill this land with the Father's glory;
> Blaze, Spirit, blaze,
> Set our hearts on fire.
> Flow, river, flow,
> Flood the nations with grace and mercy;
> Send forth Your word, Lord,
> And let there be light.
>
> Lord, I come to Your awesome presence,
> From the shadows into Your radiance;
> By the blood I may enter Your brightness,

Search me, try me, consume all my darkness.
Shine on me, shine on me.

As we gaze on Your kingly brightness
So our faces display Your likeness,
Ever changing from glory to glory,
Mirrored here may our lives tell Your story.
Shine on me, shine on me.

Our prayer is that through this book, as you read and pray and study the Bible, you will find yourself believing more deeply in the God who is fire and light, Father, Son and Holy Spirit.

SHELAGH BROWN AND GAVIN REID

PART ONE

PART ONE

1. God the Father

Some friends of mine used to have a much-loved boxer dog called Etta, and one summer Etta had seven puppies – Rosetta, Henrietta, Lambretta and Carburetta – and I forget the names of the other three, but they all ended in Etta – like their mother.

They all had names like her and they all looked like her – much smaller versions, but with the same squashed-up noses and beautiful, ugly faces. When I went to see them I was taken into the back garden, where Etta was stretched out in the sun on the grass looking pleased with herself. Her puppies were clambering all over her, playing and nestling and feeding. But even if Etta hadn't been there I would have known that those puppies were boxers. I could see it simply by looking at them.

When we see any creature we can tell what its parents were. Rabbits have baby rabbits; sparrows have baby sparrows; and we have baby human beings – and all the babies grow up to be like their parents. Not the spitting image of them. They are not copies. Yet we can see what they are without any trouble at all.

But when Jesus says 'He who has seen me has seen the Father', he is using our human understanding of the way things are to lead us into a profound understanding of the mystery and the nature of God. It is not that the Father *looks* like Jesus, but that the way Jesus was in himself is the way God is – and that everything Jesus did and said is utterly in line with the character of God. So to know what Jesus is like is to know what God is like. To see the Son is to see the Father.

Jesus lived the whole of his life in a personal relationship with the Father – and he showed us the nature of God the Father.

Theologians spend most of their time exploring the nature of God. Sometimes their public utterances and their books are a bit beyond us and we start to get worried. Perhaps we haven't got it right? Perhaps it is too difficult for us to believe?

The trouble is that theologians often talk about God in conceptual terms instead of personal ones. They say that he is 'omniscient', 'omnipotent' and 'omnipresent' – which isn't a great deal of help to most of us.

There is a true story told of a professor of theology in the University of Cambridge who had to preach a sermon to the college servants. They all sat there in the college chapel waiting – the cooks and the kitchenmaids, the cleaners and the bedmakers. The first part of the service was over and now it was time for the sermon. The learned theologian climbed up into the pulpit and began: 'I have no doubt that you will have been giving much thought to the ontological argument for the existence of God . . .'

We, of course, know perfectly well (don't we?!) that the word 'ontological' means 'relating to, or based upon, being or existence' (though I have just looked it up in Webster's Dictionary to make sure I had it *absolutely* right!). But it is unlikely that many of the theologian's congregation were absolutely clear what it meant.

4

Fortunately for us, Jesus did things rather differently. He told us
what God is like by telling us a story about a father who had two
sons: a son who went away into a far country but then came
home again, and a son who stayed at home but never really
enjoyed all the benefits of his father's company.

There was a man who had two sons. The younger one said to his father,
'Father, give me my share of the estate.' So he divided his property
between them.

    Not long after that, the younger son got together all he had, set off for
a distant country and there squandered his wealth in wild living. After
he had spent everything, there was a severe famine in that whole country,
and he began to be in need. So he went and hired himself out to a citizen
of that country, who sent him to his fields to feed pigs. He longed to fill
his stomach with the pods that the pigs were eating, but no one gave
him anything.

Luke 15:11–32 NIV

When he came to his senses, he said, 'How many of my father's hired men have food to spare, and here I am starving to death! I will set out and go back to my father and say to him: Father, I have sinned against heaven and against you. I am no longer worthy to be called your son; make me like one of your hired men. So he got up and went to his father.

But while he was still a long way off, his father saw him and was filled with compassion for him; he ran to his son, threw his arms around him and kissed him.

The son said to him, 'Father, I have sinned against heaven and against you. I am no longer worthy to be called your son.'

But the father said to his servants, 'Quick! Bring the best robe and put it on him. Put a ring on his finger and sandals on his feet. Bring the fattened calf and kill it. Let's have a feast and celebrate. For this son of mine was dead and is alive again; he was lost and is found.' So they began to celebrate.

Meanwhile, the older son was in the field. When he came near the house, he heard music and dancing. So he called one of the servants and asked him what was going on. 'Your brother has come,' he replied, 'and your father has killed the fattened calf because he has him back safe and sound.'

The older brother became angry and refused to go in. So his father went out and pleaded with him. But he answered his father, 'Look! All these years I've been slaving for you and I never disobeyed your orders. Yet you never gave me even a young goat so I could celebrate with my friends. But when this son of yours who has squandered your property with prostitutes comes home, you kill the fattened calf for him!'

'My son,' the father said, 'you are always with me, and everything I have is yours. But we have to celebrate and be glad, because this brother of yours was dead and is alive again; he was lost and is found.'

We usually talk about that story as the parable of the Prodigal Son. But a famous German preacher and theologian, Helmut Thielicke, called it the parable of the Waiting Father, because it is the father who is right at the heart of it. It is the father's heart that aches when his younger son leaves home, and it is the father who waits and longs for him to come back again. It is the father who says to his elder son, 'Son, you are always with me, and everything I have is yours.'

Jesus told us that story to tell us what our Father God is like. But Jesus did more than tell us stories about the Father. He showed him to us. And he said that if we really knew him we would also know his Father:

'I am the way and the truth and the life. No one comes to the Father John 14:6–9 NIV except through me. If you really knew me, you would know my Father as well. From now on, you do know him and have seen him.'

Philip said, 'Lord, show us the Father and that will be enough for us.'

Jesus answered, 'Don't you know me, Philip, even after I have been among you such a long time? Anyone who has seen me has seen the Father . . .'

They could know what the Father was like because they had seen the Son.

To be a Christian is to be one of the sons and daughters of God, a child of God the Father. Jesus said we had to be 'born again', and that is to experience (not always consciously) a second birth after our first birth. He told Nicodemus about the necessity of it: 'I tell you the truth, no one can see the kingdom of God unless he is born again' (John 3:3 NIV).

The first birth is physical. The second birth is spiritual, and the crucial thing about it is that we have a different Father. A person may not be able to remember their second birth. We only ever remember our first one in the throes of psychotherapy or in the process of an inner healing. But if we know in our heart that God is our Father then we can be sure that our second birth has taken place. We are at home in the Father's house, and we call God our Father. And it all happens through the Son.

When the time had fully come, God sent his Son, born of a woman, born Galatians 4:4–6 NIV under law, to redeem those under law, that we might receive the full rights of sons. Because you are sons, God sent the Spirit of his Son into our hearts, the Spirit who calls out, '*Abba*, Father.'

Christianity says that God the Father loves the world and that God the Son died for it:

For God so loved the world that he gave his one and only Son, that John 3:16 NIV whoever believes in him shall not perish but have eternal life.

The word for 'Father', which the earliest Christians learnt from Jesus . . . was the intimate mode of address from child to father . . . We must suppose that Jesus used it, by choice, because it is the appropriate way of speaking about the personal life with God which was his concern . . .

7

He was aware that there were sophisticated types who could not take his teaching . . .

'I thank thee, Father,' he is recorded to have said, 'for hiding these things from the learned and wise, and revealing them to the simple . . .' And again, 'Unless you turn round and become like children, you will never enter the kingdom of God . . .'

This 'turning round' is a large part of what is meant by 'repentance' in the gospels. It is learning to think of God as your Father and of yourself as his child, quite simply.

C. H. Dodd, The Founder of Christianity

Group material, prayers and meditation for chapter 1:
GOD THE FATHER

1. Read out quite slowly the Bible passage about the Waiting Father on pages 5–6 – and ask people as they listen to think about the father's feelings. Have a short silence afterwards (tell the group beforehand that this will happen).
2. Discuss any particular things that have struck you afresh, or perhaps for the first time, in the Bible reading or in this chapter.
3. Discuss the verbs 'to father' and 'to mother'. Think of them in human terms – and then draw the lines back to God.
4. Jesus is the Son. So what does that tell us and show us about the Father?

Meditation

[*Note to leader: Have a silence in between each phrase.*]
Shut your eyes – and be quiet for a few moments . . .

Remember that you are a child . . . however old you are . . .
Remember your own parents . . . your father . . . your mother . . .
You are a human being – like them . . .
Think about Mary – the mother of Jesus . . .
Think about God – the Father of Jesus . . .
Think about Jesus – 'truly God and truly man' . . .
Think about Jesus' words – 'He who has seen me has seen the Father' . . .
Think of the disciples' words: 'Lord, show us the Father' . . .
Think of the Waiting Father, waiting for his son to come home . . .

He got up and went to his father. But while he was still a long way off, his father saw him and was filled with compassion for him; he ran to his son, threw his arms around him and kissed him. The son said to him 'Father, I have sinned against heaven and against you. I am no longer worthy to be called your son.' But the father said to his servants, 'Quick! Bring the best robe and put it on him. Put a ring on his finger and sandals on his feet. Bring the fattened calf and kill it. Let's have a feast and celebrate. For this son of mine was dead and is alive again; he was lost and is found.'

Think of the elder son, at home all the time, but not appreciating it . . .

Think of that from the Father's point of view . . . the disappointment of it . . . Remember what he said to him: 'Son, you are always with me, and all that is mine is yours . . .'

Have a short silence. Then ask people to pray their own prayers.

Finish by praying the Lord's Prayer together.

2. God the Son

Gavin and Mary Reid have three children and sometimes Gavin finds himself looking at them in astonishment – because as he looks he can see both himself and Mary. He finds it uncanny – because he doesn't only see the likeness in their faces but also in their character traits. And, as he says ruefully, 'They aren't always the best!'

Children are like their parents, and the Son of God is like God the Father. The New Testament says that to see Jesus the Son is to see God the Father. It is to see the glory of God. St Paul talks about 'the glory of Christ, who is the likeness of God', and says both what the content of Christian preaching ought to be and what it means to be a Christian:

2 Corinthians 4:5–6 RSV What we preach is not ourselves, but Jesus Christ as Lord, with ourselves as your servants for Jesus' sake. For it is the God who said, 'Let light shine out of darkness,' who has shone in our hearts to give the light of the knowledge of the glory of God in the face of Christ.

The glory of God

The glory of a thing or a person is its nature, shining out of it for everyone to see. A cherry tree covered in white blossom in the

10

springtime. A shy, spotted deer trotting up the side of a field. A lake of shining water with swallows skimming over it. A tiny, newborn baby, with its ten little fingers and ten little toes in perfect miniature, so that it moves us to wonder every time we look.

When Paul is explaining what our resurrection bodies are going to be like, he does it by starting with the glory of the bodies that we already know and goes on from there:

What you sow is not the body which is to be, but a bare kernel, perhaps **1 Corinthians** of wheat or of some other grain. But God gives it a body as he has **15:37–42 RSV** chosen, and to each kind of seed its own body. For not all flesh is alike, but there is one kind for men, another for animals, another for birds, and another for fish. There are celestial bodies and there are terrestrial bodies; but the glory of the celestial is one, and the glory of the terrestrial is another. There is one glory of the sun, and another glory of the moon, and another glory of the stars; for star differs from star in glory. So is it with the resurrection of the dead . . .

When the followers of Jesus looked at him they could see a man. But he made an astonishing claim. He said that to see him was also to have seen the Father. They didn't see clearly and they didn't understand immediately. He had to take them by the hand and lead them there, gently showing them the way one step at a time. This particular claim was the climax of what he said to comfort them just a few days before his death:

'Let not your hearts be troubled; believe in God, believe also in me. In **John 14:1–11** my Father's house are many rooms; if it were not so, would I have told **RSV** you that I go to prepare a place for you? And when I go and prepare a place for you, I will come again and will take you to myself, that where I am you may be also. And you know the way where I am going.' Thomas said to him, 'Lord, we do not know where you are going; how can we know the way?' Jesus said to him, 'I am the way, and the truth, and the life; no one comes to the Father, but by me. If you had known me, you would have known my Father also; henceforth you know him and have seen him.'
Philip said to him, 'Lord, show us the Father, and we shall be satisfied.' Jesus said to him, 'Have I been with you so long, and yet you do not know me, Philip? He who has seen me has seen the Father; how can you say, "Show us the Father"? Do you not believe that I am in the Father

11

and the Father in me? The words that I say to you I do not speak on my own authority; but the Father who dwells in me does his works. Believe me that I am in the Father and the Father in me; or else believe me for the sake of the works themselves."

What is God like?

The answer to the question, 'What is God like?' is, 'Like Jesus. Look at him. Look at the things he does and the way he relates to people.' So when we look, what do we see?

What we *don't* see is a God who sits a long way above the world with a disapproving look on his face. Rather, we see a God who is down here with us – and attracted to sinners as steel is attracted to a magnet. 'Those who are well have no need of a physician, but those who are sick; I came not to call the righteous, but sinners' (Mark 2:17 RSV).

'Accept that you are accepted' was how a theologian called Paul Tillich once summed up the gospel; and accepting people just as they were was exactly what Jesus did – swindlers and prostitutes and all. He let one prostitute kiss his feet and cry all over them, and then dry them with her hair – which she had flowing loose to show what she was. But Jesus saw *who* she was – a human being made in the image of God.

Luke 7:36–48
RSV

One of the Pharisees asked him to eat with him, and he went into the Pharisee's house, and took his place at table. And behold, a woman of the city, who was a sinner, when she learned that he was at table in the Pharisee's house, brought an alabaster flask of ointment, and standing behind him at his feet, weeping, she began to wet his feet with her tears, and wiped them with the hair of her head, and kissed his feet, and anointed them with the ointment.

Now when the Pharisee who had invited him saw it, he said to himself, 'If this man were a prophet, he would have known who and what sort of woman this is who is touching him, for she is a sinner.' And Jesus answering said to him, 'Simon, I have something to say to you.' And he answered, 'What is it, Teacher?' 'A certain creditor had two debtors; one owed five hundred denarii, and the other fifty. When they could not pay, he forgave them both. Now which of them will love him more?'

12

Simon answered, 'The one, I suppose, to whom he forgave more.' And he said to him, 'You have judged rightly.'

Then turning toward the woman he said to Simon, 'Do you see this woman? I entered your house, you gave me no water for my feet, but she has wet my feet with her tears and wiped them with her hair. You gave me no kiss, but from the time I came in she has not ceased to kiss my feet. You did not anoint my head with oil, but she has anointed my feet with ointment. Therefore I tell you, her sins, which are many, are forgiven, for she loved much; but he who is forgiven little, loves little.' And he said to her, 'Your sins are forgiven.'

A few years ago I went to look at the pictures in the Courtauld Gallery in London. One of the paintings is by Toulouse Lautrec, and the moment I saw it I was transfixed. It is called 'The tête-à-tête supper', and a woman with a hideously raddled, painted face is sitting next to a man at a table. But you can't see his face. It is turned away, so that we don't know who he is. Probably the woman didn't know either, not very well. Her face is like a mask: grotesque – painted white, like a clown, with gashes of scarlet. And she is smiling.

When I looked at the picture I hated it, and perhaps Toulouse Lautrec meant me to – in the superb art that makes us look right to the heart of things and see them as they really are. To look at that picture is to feel all the pain of a sordid pleasure: the thing which we desperately wish in the heart of us was different – the way we'd always wanted it to be.

When I looked it made me remember that the woman in the picture had been a child once, and that she had looked out at the world with those beautiful, clear eyes that children have; not just some children – all of them. Hoping for happiness and love. But this one had ended up in the back room of a brothel, with a man she didn't know.

The picture of a man and a woman, both made in the image of God – and the image marred and spoilt and broken. But it's mendable. And what will mend it is love. The love of God that we can see in a man – a man who would have been perfectly at home with the two in Toulouse Lautrec's painting, sitting at the table and eating with them.

Jesus said, 'The Son of man has come eating and drinking; and you say, 'Behold, a glutton and a drunkard, a friend of tax collectors and sinners!' Yet wisdom is justified by all her children' (Luke 7:34, 35 RSV).

'No one has ever seen God', writes St John. But he doesn't stop there. He goes on: 'The only Son, who is in the bosom of the Father, he has made him known' (John 1:18 RSV).

The Word

The Prologue to the Gospel of John tells us who the Son is, and this is the great passage that is so often read out in churches at Christmas, telling of the mystery of the incarnation:

John 1:1–14
RSV

In the beginning was the Word, and the Word was with God, and the Word was God. He was in the beginning with God; all things were made through him, and without him was not anything made that was made. In him was life, and the life was the light of men. The light shines in the darkness, and the darkness has not overcome it.

There was a man sent from God, whose name was John. He came for testimony, to bear witness to the light, that all might believe through him. He was not the light, but came to bear witness to the light.

The true light that enlightens every man was coming into the world. He was in the world, and the world was made through him, yet the world knew him not. He came to his own home, and his own people received him not. But to all who received him, who believed in his name, he gave power to become children of God; who were born, not of blood nor of the will of the flesh nor of the will of man, but of God.

And the Word became flesh and dwelt among us, full of grace and truth; we have beheld his glory, glory as of the only Son from the Father.

The Word in creation

For the Jew, the Word was God, and the world was created by the word of God. God spoke his creative word in the darkness, and the heavens (the galaxies spinning round in space) came into

14

existence – and then, finally, men and women like us, being created by the God of love to have a relationship with him for ever. The Jew John is saying that a personal energy went forth from God which was God, yet not God the Father but God the Son – the Word.

In *The Magician's Nephew* by C. S. Lewis there is a marvellous account of how Aslan creates Narnia, not by speaking a word, but by singing:

The Lion was pacing to and fro about that empty land and singing his new song. It was softer and more lilting than the song by which he had called up the stars and the sun; a gentle, rippling music. And as he walked and sang the valley grew green with grass. It spread out from the Lion like a pool. It ran up the sides of the little hills like a wave. In a few minutes it was creeping up the lower slopes of the distant mountains, making that young world every moment softer . . .

'All things were made through him', John is saying, 'and without him was not anything made that was made.' Quite a claim! And it was made by a Jew, who knew that 'the Lord our God is one Lord . . .'

He can make us into God's children

John also says that the one he is writing about can give us power to become children of God, if we will believe in him and receive him. He is the only Son of the Father, unique. But he can make us into the sons and daughters of God. We can be 'born again' into the family of God – and call God our Father, our *'abba'* or 'daddy', as Jesus did. Paul says that God's plan for us is that we should be 'conformed to the image of his Son', so that 'he might be the first-born among many brethren' (Romans 8:29 RSV).

The letter to the Hebrews says: 'It was fitting that he, for whom and by whom all things exist, in bringing many sons to glory, should make the pioneer of their salvation perfect through suffering' (Hebrews 2:10 RSV). That letter begins by telling us about the uniqueness of the Son:

Hebrews 1:1–3
RSV
In many and various ways God spoke of old to our fathers by the prophets; but in these last days he has spoken to us by a Son, whom he appointed the heir of all things, through whom also he created the world. He reflects the glory of God and bears the very stamp of his nature, upholding the universe by his word of power. When he had made purification for sins, he sat down at the right hand of the Majesty on high . . .

The writer is saying that Jesus bears the very stamp of God's nature. He is like a seal that people stamp in wax and then seal on a document – and what is then seen is the exact impression of the original seal. He is also the shining out of the glory, or the character of God. God is just like Jesus. Jesus is the Word of God and has the very nature of God.

What really clinched the matter for the first followers of Jesus was the resurrection. Paul sets it out at the start of his great letter to the Christians in Rome, and at the same time tells about God's purpose for himself, for them (and for us) and for all the nations of the world:

Romans 1:1–7
RSV
Paul, a servant of Jesus Christ, called to be an apostle, set apart for the gospel of God which he promised beforehand through his prophets in the holy scriptures, the gospel concerning his Son, who was descended from David according to the flesh and designated Son of God in power according to the Spirit of holiness by his resurrection from the dead,

Jesus Christ our Lord, through whom we have received grace and apostleship to bring about the obedience of faith for the sake of his name among all the nations, including yourselves who are called to belong to Jesus Christ; to all God's beloved in Rome, who are called to be saints: Grace to you and peace from God our Father and the Lord Jesus Christ.

Group material, meditation and prayers for chapter 2:
GOD THE SON

1. Read out John 14:1–11 and follow it with a short time of silence.
2. Discuss the points that have particularly struck you in that Bible passage and in this chapter.
3. Ask people what it means to them that Jesus is the Son and that to see him is to see the Father.
4. Ask each person to say briefly one thing that the passage means to them.

Meditation

[*Note to leader: Tell people that you are going to start with a silence, and then read out the start of Paul's letter to the Romans very slowly. Ask them to listen attentively to the words, and to ask God to speak to them through the words . . .*]
Read Romans 1:1–7

A Prayer from the Scottish Prayer Book

Almighty God, who at the baptism of thy blessed Son Jesus Christ in the river Jordan didst manifest his glorious Godhead; Grant, we beseech thee, that the brightness of his presence may shine in our hearts, and his glory be set forth in our lives, through the same Jesus Christ our Lord.

An Orthodox Prayer

O Christ my Saviour, the enlightenment of those who lie in darkness, the salvation of all in despair, I seek thee early in the morning: enlighten me with thy brightness, O King of peace, for I know no other God save thee.

A Prayer from 'Shine, Jesus, Shine'

> Lord, the light of Your love is shining
> In the midst of the darkness, shining;
> Jesus, Light of the World, shine upon us,
> Set us free by the truth You now bring us,
> Shine on me, shine on me . . .

Ask people to pray their own prayers out loud.

Finish by praying the Lord's Prayer together.

3. God the Holy Spirit

The first Christians' experience of God was so real and so powerful that they were driven to describe it in ways that sounded blasphemous to the orthodox Jewish religion out of which Christianity sprang. The early Jewish Christians, who had known and believed from their childhood that there was one God and that God was one, spoke and wrote in a way that sounded as if they now believed they had encountered God in two other persons: in Jesus and in the Holy Spirit.

The Trinity

That experience of God as 'one in three and three in one', which we call the doctrine of the Trinity, was not produced by the early church as the result of long theological discussions or hours of abstract theological thought. They talked about it and wrote about it because they were aware that God had acted and revealed himself not just in one way, or even two, but three. In addition, Jesus had talked to them about it, although it took them a long time to understand. It was their experience of God the Holy Spirit which finally led them into the truth.

Later on, the church began to wrestle with the concept of the Trinity, and argued passionately about its metaphysics. The church is *still* arguing! In the fourth century they set it down in tightly worded definitions of what they believed it did and didn't mean. The church then talked of 'the doctrine of the Trinity,' of which the Father was the first person, Jesus the second person, and the Holy Spirit the third person.

The early church, however, had spoken about it much more loosely and far more experientially, so many of us will find the New Testament accounts easier to understand than theological accounts of the nature of the Godhead.

'You will see me again'

The New Testament says that after the resurrection appearances of Jesus he went away, but that his disciples then knew him in another way that was apparently even better than before. In John's gospel Jesus tells his disciples that he is going to leave them but that he will come back to them again: 'I am telling you the truth: it is better for you that I go away, because if I do not go, the Helper will not come to you' (John 16:7 GNB).

But how could it possibly be better if he went away? The great delight of a personal relationship is to be with the person we love. When we have been separated from a friend or a lover we greet them by hugging them and saying, 'How good it is to see you! I have missed you.' And when we part again we look forward to the next time we shall see them.

John says that the disciples were bewildered.

John 16:16–8
RSV

'A little while, and you will see me no more; again a little while, and you will see me.' Some of his disciples said to one another, 'What is this that he says to us, "A little while, and you will not see me, and again a little while, and you will see me"; and, "because I go to the Father"?' They

20

said, 'What does he mean by "a little while"? We do not know what he means.'

But later on they did know. The agony of the parting came on Good Friday and in the hopelessness of the next day. Then, in the glory of the first Easter morning, the wonder of the resurrection dawned on them. On that day, and for forty days more, he appeared to them many times in ways 'that proved beyond doubt that he was alive' (Acts 1:3 GNB).

After that, the New Testament says, he went away into heaven. Soon after that the disciples became aware that God was with them in an even better way. The account in the second chapter of the Acts of the Apostles of the strange happenings on the Day of Pentecost says that God descended upon his people in the person and power of the Holy Spirit.

The Holy Spirit

Charles Williams, a friend and contemporary of C. S. Lewis, dedicated his book *The Descent of the Dove: an account of the Holy Spirit in the Church*, to 'the companions of the co-inherence' – and he meant by that all Christians. The word co-inherence means 'existing with, or in'. Iron and fire can co-inhere with each other. The iron does not cease to be iron nor the fire to be fire: what happens is that the iron is aglow with the fire.

The New Testament says that the Holy Spirit descended in a rushing mighty wind and in tongues of fire – and it exhorts us to 'be aglow' with the Spirit. We can, if we like, resist, and then we shall not be aglow with the Spirit and on fire for God and with God. We shall be dull embers, like a fire that never got going or else died down – and no one will be attracted through us to God.

Wind, fire and water

The New Testament writers used a rich variety of imagery to describe their experience of the Spirit. He was like wind, water

21

and fire – all traditional symbols of the presence of God with his people.

The wind of God had moved over the face of the waters on the first day of creation. The water of life had streamed like a river from the throne of God in Ezekiel's vision (Ezekiel chapter 47). A pillar of fire had guided the Jews out of their slavery in Egypt into the freedom of the promised land (Exodus 13:20–21). God was like wind and water and fire. In another, far profounder way, God was also like Jesus.

The name they gave to Jesus was Emmanuel, which means 'God with us'. The Holy Spirit was 'God with us' too, and in an even better way. First those early Christians were aware of God. Then of God-in-manhood in the person of Jesus Christ. Then, finally, of God within themselves. Charles Williams described the glory of the transition in a dramatic and unusual way:

There had appeared in Palestine . . . a certain being. This being was in the form of a man, a peripatetic teacher . . . There were plenty of that sort about, springing up in the newly-established peace of the Empire. But this one had a higher potential of power, and a much more distracting method. It had a very effective verbal style, notably in imprecation, together with a recurrent ambiguity of statement. It continually scored debating-points over its interlocutors. It agreed with everything on the one hand, and denounced everything on the other.

For example it said nothing against the Roman occupation; it urged obedience to the Jewish hierarchy; it proclaimed holiness to the Lord. But it was present at doubtfully holy feasts; it associated with rich men and loose women; it commented acerbly on the habits of the hierarchy; and while encouraging everyone to pay their debts, it radiated a general disapproval, or at least doubt, of every kind of property . . .

It said it could control anything and yet had to submit to everything. It said its Father in Heaven would do anything it wished, but that for itself it would do nothing but what its Father in heaven wished. And it promised that when it disappeared, it would cause some other Power to illumine, confirm, and direct that small group of stupefied and helpless followers whom it deigned, with the sounds of the rush of a sublime tenderness, to call its friends.

It did disappear – either by death or burial, as its opponents held, or, as its followers afterwards asserted, by some later and less usual method. Those followers at any rate remained, according to all the evidence, in a small secret group in Jerusalem. They supposed themselves to be waiting for the new manifestation which they had been promised, in order that they might take up the work which their Lord had left them. According to their own evidence, the manifestation came.

At a particular moment, and by no means secretly, the heavenly Secrets opened upon them, and there was communicated to that group of Jews, in a rush of wind and dazzle of tongued flames, the secret of the Paraclete in the Church. Our Lord Messiah had vanished in his flesh; our Lord the Spirit expressed himself towards the flesh and spirit of the disciples. The Church, itself one of the Secrets, began to be.

(The Descent of the Dove)

Called in to help

'Paraclete' comes from the greek word *parakletos*, which really means 'someone who is called in'. The Bible commentator William Barclay says that a *parakletos* is always *'someone called in to help* when the person who calls him in is in trouble or distress or doubt or bewilderment'. He 'might be a person *called in* to give witness in a law court in someone's favour; he might be an advocate *called in* to plead someone's cause when someone was under a charge which would issue in serious penalty; he might be an expert *called in* to give advice in some difficult situation. He might be a person *called in* when, for example, a company of soldiers were depressed and dispirited to put new courage into their minds and hearts' (William Barclay, *The Gospel of John*).

Some Bibles translate the word as 'comforter', and the first person to do that was Wycliffe in the fourteenth century. But that word meant more in his day than it does in ours. We think of a comforter as someone who lifts up our spirits when we are sad. But there is a much stronger meaning than that. The word 'comfort' is derived from two Latin words – *'con'* meaning with, and *'fortis'* meaning strong. In the Bayeux Tapestry one of the pictures has William the Conqueror standing behind a small company of his troops and prodding them with a lance to make them go forward. The caption underneath (when translated) reads, 'William comforteth his troops'!

God with us

The Holy Spirit is God-with-us just as Jesus was God-with-us. We could say that the Holy Spirit is God's invisible man; but however we think about the Spirit we have to get away from any idea of just some vague power, or a sort of floating ghost.

In the gospel of John Jesus says:

John 14:15–17
RSV
If you love me, you will keep my commandments. And I will pray the Father, and he will give you another Counsellor, to be with you for ever, even the Spirit of truth, whom the world cannot receive, because it neither sees him nor knows him; you know him, for he dwells with you, and will be in you.

But when the Spirit comes to us then Jesus comes to us. The passage goes on:

Verses 18–20
RSV
I will not leave you desolate; I will come to you. Yet a little while, and the world will see me no more, but you will see me; because I live, you will live also. In that day you will know that I am in my Father, and you in me, and I in you.

Jesus is teaching us and telling us about a mystical and spiritual mutual indwelling of the three persons of the one God with each other and with us. When the Spirit comes to us so also do the Father and the Son:

Verse 23 RSV
If a man loves me, he will keep my word, and my Father will love him, and we will come to him and make our home with him.

Christianity is essentially a mystical religion, and all Christians are indwelt by God – even though some of us may only allow him to enter a little way into our hearts and not into the depths of them.

God's Spirit and our bodies

But Christianity is also deeply concerned with the body. One day it will be raised from the dead and be changed from mortality into immortality. And the indwelling of God the Holy Spirit in us is the reason why it matters what we do (or don't do) with our bodies.

24

The body is not meant for immorality, but for the Lord, and the Lord for the body. And God raised the Lord and will also raise us up by his power. Do you not know that your bodies are members of Christ? Shall I therefore take the members of Christ and make them members of a prostitute? Never! Do you not know that he who joins himself to a prostitute becomes one body with her? For, as it is written, 'The two shall become one flesh.' But he who is united to the Lord becomes one spirit with him.

Shun immorality. Every other sin which a man commits is outside the body; but the immoral man sins against his own body. Do you not know that your body is a temple of the Holy Spirit within you, which you have from God? You are not your own; you were bought with a price. So glorify God in your body.'

1 Corinthians 6:13–20 RSV

The Spirit and the 'flesh'

The great chapter 8 of Paul's letter to the Romans has more to say about the work of the Holy Spirit in us:

There is therefore now no condemnation for those who are in Christ Jesus. For the law of the Spirit of life in Christ Jesus has set me free from the law of sin and death. For God has done what the law, weakened by the flesh, could not do: sending his own Son in the likeness of sinful flesh and for sin, he condemned sin in the flesh, in order that the just requirement of the law might be fulfilled in us, who walk not according to the flesh but according to the Spirit. For those who live according to the flesh set their minds on the things of the flesh, but those who live according to the Spirit set their minds on the things of the Spirit. To set the mind on the flesh is death, but to set the mind on the Spirit is life and peace. For the mind that is set on the flesh is hostile to God; it does not submit to God's law, indeed it cannot; and those who are in the flesh cannot please God.

Romans 8:1–8 RSV

['When Paul uses the word "flesh" in this way, he really means human nature in all its weakness, its impotence and its helplessness. He means human nature in its vulnerability to sin and to temptation. He means that part of man which gives sin its chance and its bridgehead. He means sinful human nature, apart from Christ and apart from God. He means everything that attaches a man to the world instead of God' (William Barclay, *Romans*).]

But you are not in the flesh, you are in the Spirit, if in fact the Spirit of God dwells in you. Any one who does not have the Spirit of Christ does not belong to him. But if Christ is in you, although your bodies are dead because of sin, your spirits are alive because of righteousness. If the

Romans 8:9–16 RSV

25

Spirit of him who raised Jesus from the dead dwells in you, he who raised Christ Jesus from the dead will give life to your mortal bodies also through his Spirit which dwells in you.

So then, brethren, we are debtors, not to the flesh, to live according to the flesh – for if you live according to the flesh you will die, but if by the Spirit you put to death the deeds of the body you will live. For all who are led by the Spirit of God are sons of God. For you did not receive the spirit of slavery to fall back into fear, but you have received the spirit of sonship. When we cry, 'Abba, Father!' it is the Spirit himself bearing witness with our spirit that we are children of God . . .

Group material, meditation and prayers for chapter 3:
GOD THE HOLY SPIRIT

1. Read out the verses from John's gospel (14:15–20 and 23) together with the connecting comments (page 24).
2. Ask each person to say what that means to them and also what the Holy Spirit means to them.
3. Continue reading aloud from this chapter, following immediately after John 14:23, from 'Christianity is essentially a mystical religion . . .' down to the end of 1 Corinthians 6:13–20.
4. Ask people if they think of their body as a temple of the Holy Spirit. If not, how could they start to do so and to believe in the wonder of it?

Meditation

Start with a silence. Then read out the passage from Romans 8:1–16 very slowly, and ask people to listen and to pray that God will speak to them through it and show them what it means.

Collect for Pentecost, Book of Common Prayer

God, who as at this time didst teach the hearts of thy faithful people, by the sending to them the light of thy Holy Spirit; Grant us by the same Spirit to have a right judgement in all things, and evermore to rejoice in his holy comfort; through the merits of Christ Jesus our Saviour, who liveth and reigneth with thee, in the unity of the same Spirit, one God, world without end.   Amen

A Prayer from 'Shine, Jesus, Shine'

> Shine, Jesus, shine,
> Fill this land with the Father's glory;
> Blaze, Spirit, blaze,
> Set our hearts on fire.
> Flow, river, flow,
> Flood the nations with grace and mercy;
> Send forth Your word, Lord,
> And let there be light.

Have a time of silence. Then ask people to pray their own prayers aloud.

Finish by praying the Lord's Prayer together.

4. Sons and Daughters of God

In a well known fairy story a princess allows a frog to sleep on her pillow, and when they wake up in the morning he has been transformed into the prince that he really is.

Transformation

Christianity is also in the business of transforming us – and it isn't a fairy story and the transformation is a total one. We are changed from being the sons and daughters of Adam into the sons and daughters of the living God. We are a new creation, and it happens through Christ. Paul writes to the Christians in Corinth about what happens and about his own ministry:

Therefore, if anyone is in Christ, he is a new creation; the old has gone, the new has come! All this is from God, who reconciled us to himself through Christ and gave us the ministry of reconciliation: that God was reconciling the world to himself in Christ, not counting men's sins against them. And he has committed to us the message of reconciliation. We are therefore Christ's ambassadors, as though God were making his appeal through us. We implore you on Christ's behalf: Be reconciled to God. God made him who had no sin to be sin for us, so that in him we might become the righteousness of God.

2 Corinthians 5:17–22 NIV

A little further on in the same letter Paul tells the members of the new creation how they ought to behave and who they are:

Holy living

Do not be yoked together with unbelievers. For what do righteousness and wickedness have in common? Or what fellowship can light have with darkness? What harmony is there between Christ and Belial? What does a believer have in common with an unbeliever? What agreement is there between the temple of God and idols? For we are the temple of the living God. As God has said: 'I will live with them and walk among them, and I will be their God, and they will be my people.'

2 Corinthians 6:14—7:1 NIV

> 'Therefore come out from them and be separate,
>   says the Lord.
> Touch no unclean thing, and I will receive you.'
> 'I will be a Father to you,
>   and you will be my sons and daughters,
>   says the Lord Almighty.'

Since we have these promises, dear friends, let us purify ourselves from everything that contaminates body and spirit, perfecting holiness out of reverence for God.

As his children, God calls us to live holy lives. The call is there all through the Bible, and if we will open our ears to it we shall hear it in many places and through many people.

The great revival in the eighteeneth century began when John Wesley called Christians to holy living in the midst of a corrupt society and a corrupt church. The Tractarian Movement in the Church of England began for the same reason in the nineteenth century, publishing tracts which spoke out against the corruption in society and in the church.

In this Decade of Evangelism we need to listen to that same call of God to holy living. The world will never listen to what we say unless it sees the sons and daughters of God living Christ-like, holy lives. It all starts with holiness, because God is holy and if we belong to God then so are we. William Temple, who was Archbishop of Canterbury in the 1940s, wrote this about holiness:

The primary characteristic of the Church is neither its missionary enterprise which is the essence of Apostolicity, nor its universal scope which is its Catholicity, but the fact that it is constituted by the redeeming act of God in Christ and is sustained by the indwelling divine Spirit, or in short its Holiness. And the first way in which it is called to be itself is neither through missionary extension nor through influence upon national life but through inward sanctification.

Citizen and Churchman

The beginning and the end of holiness is a relationship with our Holy God, through Christ, in the Holy Spirit. And like all relationships, we have to give time to it. An old hymn spells it out:

> Take time to be holy,
> Speak oft with thy Lord,
> Abide in Him always,
> And feed on His Word.
> Make friends of God's children,
> Help those who are weak;
> Forgetting in nothing
> His blessing to seek.
>
> Take time to be holy,
> The world rushes on;
> Spend much time in secret
> With Jesus alone.
> By looking to Jesus
> Like Him thou shalt be;
> Thy friends, in thy conduct,
> His likeness shall see.
>
> W. D. Longstaff

Paul's first letter to Timothy tells him how he ought to live (and how we ought to live) and it gives to God the Father (whose children we are if we are Christians) the title of King of kings and Lord of lords:

There is great gain in godliness with contentment; for we brought nothing into the world, and we cannot take anything out of the world; but if we have food and clothing, with these we shall be content. But those who desire to be rich fall into temptation, into a snare, into many senseless and hurtful desires that plunge men into ruin and destruction. For the love of money is the root of all evils; it is through this craving that some have wandered away from the faith and pierced their hearts with many pangs.

    But as for you, man of God, shun all this; aim at righteousness, godliness, faith, love, steadfastness, gentleness. Fight the good fight of the faith; take hold of the eternal life to which you were called when you made the good confession in the presence of many witnesses. In the presence of God who gives life to all things, and of Christ Jesus who in his testimony before Pontius Pilate made the good confession, I charge you to keep the commandment unstained and free from reproach until the appearing of our Lord Jesus Christ; and this will be made manifest at the proper time by the blessed and only Sovereign, the King of kings and Lord of lords, who alone has immortality and dwells in unapproachable light, whom no man has ever seen or can see. To him be honour and eternal dominion. Amen.

1 Timothy 6:6–16 RSV

Princes and princesses

It sometimes helps to see who we are by looking at ourselves in a different way, and using different models and images. We might like to picture our new relationship with God in Christ as making us into princes and princesses, for the simple and glorious reason that we are children of the King of kings.

As children of God we have a new status, and once we really get the fact of it into our heads it will set us free from all the feelings of inferiority that many of us suffer from (because feelings always follow from facts: never the other way round). Just one of the benefits and blessings of being a son or daughter of God is a deep healing of this sense of worthlessness and lack of value.

31

In *Nightfall,* by Christopher Bryan, Charlie Brown has called the woman he loves princess, and she writes him a letter:

Charlie Brown, I have loved you. That's a fact. And nothing can alter it. I have loved you. Weeks ago (centuries it seems) when we first met, I remember writing in my diary, 'Today Charlie called me princess.' You didn't just call me princess. You made me feel like one. Thank you, Jacquie.

But even without a Charlie or a Charlene Brown in our life to call us princess, or prince, it is still possible to know that that is what we are, and the knowledge and the certainty and the glory of it will come direct from the King of kings who is our Father.

We know that frogs are never changed into princes – and anyway frogs have their own green, spotted, leaping glory to the praise of their Creator. But there is that in us which is continually being drawn up out of ourself, to be something higher and something different. To be what we know in our heart of hearts we are meant to be.

In *The Muppet Movie* Kermit the Frog sits on a lily pad playing his little guitar and singing a song called 'The Rainbow Connection'. It is about dreams coming true, and about lovers, and about a voice that he hears calling to him.

> Have you been down the street
> And have you heard voices?
> I've heard them calling my name.
> Is this the sweet sound
> That calls the young sailor?
> The voice might be one and the same.
> I've heard it too many times to ignore it,
> It's something that I'm s'posed to be.
> Some day we'll find it, the rainbow connection,
> The lovers, the dreamers and me.

In Greek mythology the sweet sound that the sailors heard was the voice of the Sirens, luring them to destruction. The voice of God calls us to eternal life, and Jesus promised that we would recognize it when we heard it: 'The sheep hear his voice, and he calls his own sheep by name and leads them out. When he has brought out all his own, he goes before them, and the sheep follow him, for they know his voice' (John 10:3–4 RSV).

The theologian John Robinson said the same thing as Kermit the Frog, in a more learned and sophisticated way, in his book *In the End, God*. He leads into it with a quotation from the autobiography of a great Christian humanist, Nikos Kazantzakis:

'Blowing through heaven and earth, and in our hearts and the heart of every living thing, is a gigantic breath – a great Cry – which we call God. Plant life wished to continue its motionless sleep next to stagnant waters, but the Cry leaped up within it and violently shook its roots: "Away, let go of the earth, walk!" Had the tree been able to think and judge, it would have cried, "I don't want to. What are you urging me to do! You are demanding the impossible!" But the Cry, without pity, kept shaking its roots and shouting, "Away, let go of the earth, walk!"

'It shouted in this way for thousands of eons; and lo! as a result of desire and struggle, life escaped the motionless tree and was liberated. Animals appeared – worms – making themselves at home in water and mud. "We're just fine," they said. "We have peace and security; we're not budging!" But the terrible Cry hammered itself pitilessly into their loins. "Leave the mud, stand up, give birth to your betters!"

"We don't want to! We can't!"

"You can't, but I can. Stand up!"

And lo! after thousands of eons, man emerged, trembling on his still unsolid legs.'

Worms don't grow legs and trees don't walk. They never did and God never meant them to, and if we read that passage as an account of the way the Creation happened we shall miss the point of it. What we need to hear in it is the voice of God speaking to *us*.

John Robinson linked the Cry with

what the Bible speaks of as 'the call' of God, that evocative, purposive love, which not only summons men to leave the securities and satisfactions of life about them, but 'calls the generations from the beginning' (Isaiah 41:4) and indeed 'calls for the corn and increases it' (Ezekiel 36:29). But it links also with the cry of creation itself, the yearning sigh of all being for its goal, of which St Paul speaks in Romans 8:14–28.

The cry is of God's Spirit within us – and indeed within all nature – calling us constantly out of ourselves and beyond ourselves in order to be ourselves. This is one of the great classical passages of Christian eschatology [which means those things which have to do with the ultimate destiny of mankind]. It merits quoting in full from the New English Bible, because I believe that at several points this version has allowed its true meaning to stand forth for the first time, notably in making 'the Spirit' the subject of verse 28 – instead of 'all things' (KJV) or 'God' (RSV). The Spirit is here, as indeed in everything, on both sides of the relationship, taking up our inarticulate groans and translating them into prayer:

Romans 8:14–28 NEB

For all who are moved by the Spirit of God are sons of God. The Spirit you have received is not a spirit of slavery leading you back into a life of fear, but a Spirit that makes us sons, enabling us to cry 'Abba! Father!' In that cry the Spirit of God joins with our spirit in testifying that we are God's children; and if children then heirs. We are God's heirs and Christ's fellow-heirs, if we share his sufferings now in order to share his splendour hereafter.

For I reckon that the sufferings we now endure bear no comparison with the splendour, as yet unrevealed, which is in store for us. For the created universe waits with eager expectation for God's sons to be revealed. It was made the victim of frustration, not by its own choice, but because of him who made it so; yet always there was hope, because the universe itself is to be freed from the shackles of mortality and enter upon the liberty and splendour of the children of God.

Up to the present, we know, the whole created universe groans in all its parts as if in the pangs of childbirth. Not only so, but even we, to whom the Spirit is given as firstfruits of the harvest to come, are groaning inwardly while we wait for God to make us his sons and set our whole body free.

For we have been saved, though only in hope. Now to see is no longer to hope: why should a man endure and wait for what he already sees? But if we hope for something we do not yet see, then, in waiting for it, we show our endurance.

In the same way the Spirit comes to the aid of our weakness. We do not even know how we ought to pray, but through our inarticulate groans the Spirit himself is pleading for us, and God who searches our inmost being knows what the Spirit means, because he pleads for God's own people in God's own way; and in everything, as we know, he co-operates for good with those who love God and are called according to his purpose.

One of God's purposes is that the light of Christ should shine out through us into the whole world that he made and that he loves. But if the light is going to shine out of us then first of all it will have to shine into us and come into us. In Holman Hunt's painting 'The Light of the World', Christ is standing outside a house and knocking on the door. There is no handle on the outside, because if the Christ who is the light of the world is to go inside and lighten the inner darkness, then the owner of the house will have to open the door and invite him in.

Some years ago, when my life was in a mess and I was deeply unhappy, a curate called John Collins talked with me about how to put things right, and he told me about that picture. He said that if I would ask Christ into my heart he would change my life and forgive my sins. So I went home, knelt by my bed, and read out the verse which John had told me to use as I prayed: 'Behold, I stand at the door and knock; if any one hears my voice and opens the door, I will come into him and eat with him, and he with me' (Revelation 3:20 RSV).

I know that Christ did come in, because I knew with a deep certainty which nothing has ever been able to shake, that I am a child of God. I know that God is my Father, that he loves me, and that my sins are forgiven. I have sometimes prayed the same prayer since that first time – asking Christ to enter rooms in the house of my life that I had kept locked. But that first prayer totally changed my life.

Group material, meditation and prayers for chapter 4:
SONS AND DAUGHTERS OF GOD

1. Read aloud 2 Corinthians 5:17–22 and 6:14—7:1.
2. Ask everyone to say whether they know and believe that they are one of the sons and daughters of the living God.

3. Discuss what it means to be a child of God, and how we can become one and have our sins forgiven if we doubt that we are.

Meditation

Start with a time of silence.
Then pray this prayer of Archbishop Helder Camara, 'King's Son':

> Lord
> isn't your creation wasteful?
> Fruits never equal
> the seedlings' abundance.
> Springs scatter water.
> The sun gives out
> enormous light.
> May your bounty teach me
> greatness of heart.
> May your magnificence
> stop me being mean.
> Seeing you a prodigal
> and open-handed giver
> let me give unstintingly
> like a king's son
> like God's own.

Then read out Romans 8:14–28 very slowly and prayerfully, with pauses between the sentences.
Pray: 'Father, please send your Holy Spirit into our hearts, to make us your children, to make us cry out to you, "Abba! Father!" May your Spirit make us to know that we are your children – if we are. If some of us aren't, then show us that too, so that we might come to you. So that you might come to us, and forgive us our sins, and live in our hearts, through Jesus Christ, our Lord and our Saviour.   Amen'

Have a short time of silence.

Then ask people to pray their own prayers out loud.

Finish by praying the Lord's Prayer together.

5. Being Christ in the World

At the start of this book you will find the words of Graham Kendrick's song 'Shine, Jesus, shine'. The chorus of it is a prayer that through the shining he will fill the land with the Father's glory and set our own hearts on fire. But all the verses are specific prayers for different aspects of our own lives. Because unless we get those right we shall quench the Spirit and dim the shining.

> Lord, the light of Your love is shining
> In the midst of the darkness, shining;
> Jesus, Light of the World, shine upon us,
> Set us free by the truth You now bring us,
> Shine on me, shine on me.

But the truth will only set us free if we know it and allow it to change us. We have to give ourselves to God and to be prepared to change our minds.

I appeal to you therefore, brethren, by the mercies of God, to present your bodies as a living sacrifice, holy and acceptable to God, which is your spiritual worship. Do not be conformed to this world but be

Romans 12:1–2 RSV

37

transformed by the renewal of your mind, that you may prove what is the will of God, what is good and acceptable and perfect.

Garbage in, garbage out!

Our minds are a bit like computers, and what they say about computers also applies to minds: 'Garbage in, garbage out!' If our minds are programmed with false information then we have to reprogram them with the truth – because what we do grows out of what we believe. We shall not be able totally to wipe out the old information, but as we live a new life in the power of the Holy Spirit we can make sure that we don't live by the former.

The method by which we reprogram and transform our minds is

by listening to the truth of God and accepting it. We shall listen to God as we read the Bible and study it. We shall listen as we pray – not talking endlessly but making sure that we spend quite a lot of time in silence, learning to listen. We shall listen to God through the ministry of the Word in church. We shall go to Holy Communion and let the gift of God himself through the bread and the wine speak to our hearts:

Draw near with faith. Receive the body of our Lord Jesus Christ which he gave for you, and his blood which he shed for you. Eat and drink in remembrance that he died for you, and feed on him in your hearts by faith with thanksgiving.

The Body of Christ

Earlier on in the Communion service there is what is known as 'The Peace', and in one form of it the truth is stated that

> We are the Body of Christ.
> In the one Spirit we were all baptized into one body.
> Let us then pursue all that makes for peace
> and builds up our common life.

The apostle Paul tells us how to build up our common life as the body of Christ and also tells us how to live:

By the grace given to me I bid every one among you not to think of himself more highly than he ought to think, but to think with sober judgment, each according to the measure of faith which God has assigned him. For as in one body we have many members, and all the members do not have the same function, so we, though many, are one body in Christ, and individually members one of another. Having gifts that differ according to the grace given to us, let us use them: if prophecy, in proportion to our faith; if service, in our serving; he who teaches, in his teaching; he who exhorts, in his exhortation; he who contributes, in liberality; he who gives aid, with zeal; he who does acts of mercy, with cheerfulness.

Let love be genuine; hate what is evil, hold fast to what is good; love one another with brotherly affection; outdo one another in showing honour. Never flag in zeal, be aglow with the Spirit, serve the Lord. Rejoice in your hope, be patient in tribulation, be constant in prayer. Contribute to the needs of the saints, practise hospitality.

Romans 12:3–21 RSV

39

Bless those who persecute you; bless and do not curse them. Rejoice with those who rejoice, weep with those who weep. Live in harmony with one another; do not be haughty, but associate with the lowly; never be conceited. Repay no one evil for evil, but take thought for what is noble in the sight of all. If possible, so far as it depends upon you, live peaceably with all. Beloved, never avenge yourselves, but leave it to the wrath of God; for it is written, 'Vengeance is mine, I will repay, says the Lord.' No, 'if your enemy is hungry, feed him; if he is thirsty, give him drink; for by so doing you will heap burning coals upon his head.' Do not be overcome by evil, but overcome evil with good.

That's quite a call to Christlike living! But we *are* the body of Christ and that means that we are Christ in the world. Teresa of Avila wrote about that startling spiritual truth, and the more we realize the truth of it the more we shall be transformed:

Christ has no body now on earth but yours;
yours are the only hands with which he can do his work,
yours are the only feet with which he can go about the world,
yours are the only eyes through which his compassion
can shine forth upon a troubled world.
Christ has no body now on earth but yours.

Perhaps one way to realize the truth of what Teresa of Avila says is for each one of us to pray every day: 'Shine, Jesus, shine . . . Let your compassion shine forth through me upon this troubled world . . .'; and for the church to pray the same prayer: 'Let your compassion shine forth through us . . .'

Doing the truth

But the compassion of Christ that shines out through us will also do things through us. The truth is something that we do.

James 2:14–17
RSV

What does it profit, my brethren, if a man says he has faith but has not works? Can his faith save him? If a brother or sister is ill-clad and in lack of daily food, and one of you says to them, 'Go in peace, be warmed and filled,' without giving them the things needed for the body, what does it profit? So faith by itself, if it has no works, is dead.

Jesus' compassion for people meant that he gave them the truth for their minds and food for their bodies:

40

As [Jesus] went ashore he saw a great throng, and he had compassion on them, because they were like sheep without a shepherd; and he began to teach them many things. And when it grew late, his disciples came to him and said, 'This is a lonely place, and the hour is now late; send them away, to go into the country and villages round about and buy themselves something to eat.' But he answered them, 'You give them something to eat.' . . . And he said to them, 'How many loaves have you? Go and see.' And when they had found out, they said, 'Five, and two fish.' Then he commanded them all to sit down by companies upon the green grass. So they sat down in groups, by hundreds and by fifties. And taking the five loaves and the two fish he looked up to heaven, and blessed, and broke the loaves, and gave them to the disciples to set before the people; and he divided the two fish among them all. And they all ate and were satisfied. And they took up twelve baskets full of broken pieces and of the fish. And those who ate the loaves were five thousand men.

Doing good

Being Christ in the world means following in his footsteps and doing the will of God. We shall speak the truth about God and we shall do the truth, which means that we shall live good lives and do good actions.

It is a curious fact that to call someone 'a do-gooder' is to say they are not doing good at all. The people at the receiving end of their do-gooding are not enjoying it – because the doers have got it wrong and it isn't 'good' that they are doing.

'Good' isn't a vague concept floating around like a cloud in the sky. To be able to say that something is good we have to know what qualities it ought to have. A 'good' strawberry is sweet and juicy and has a good flavour. A 'bad' strawberry is sour and dry and tasteless.

Some years ago, in the Institute of Advanced Legal Studies of the University of London, the woman who was its Assistant Secretary (and responsible for furnishing the new building) purchased two very expensive office chairs from a very well known shop. Soon after they were delivered the Librarian of the Institute sat on one of them and it collapsed underneath him. Two weeks later the Principal of the University sat on the other and it collapsed underneath him.

The Assistant Secretary, horrified and perplexed, wailed out, 'But it was such a good design.' But of course that is exactly what it wasn't. It was not a good chair because it lacked the absolutely essential quality of 'chairhood' – *that the chair should support the person who sits on it.*

Blueprint for behaviour

In one sense it is more complicated to say what a 'good' human being is like, and what it means really to 'do good.' But in another sense it is quite simple. A good human being is like Jesus, and Jesus is like God. And the blueprint for good human behaviour is set out in the Bible. A summary of what it should and shouldn't be (and what we should and shouldn't do) comes in Galatians:

Galatians 5:13–25 NIV

You, my brothers, were called to be free. But do not use your freedom to indulge the sinful nature; rather, serve one another in love. The entire law is summed up in a single command: 'Love your neighbour as yourself.' If you keep on biting and devouring each other, watch out or you will be destroyed by each other.

So I say, live by the Spirit, and you will not gratify the desires of the sinful nature. For the sinful nature desires what is contrary to the Spirit, and the Spirit what is contrary to the sinful nature. They are in conflict with each other, so that you do not do what you want. But if you are led by the Spirit, you are not under the law.

The acts of the sinful nature are obvious: sexual immorality, impurity and debauchery; idolatry and witchcraft; hatred, discord, jealousy, fits of rage, selfish ambition, dissensions, factions and envy; drunkenness, orgies, and the like. I warn you, as I did before, that those who live like this will not inherit the kingdom of God.

But the fruit of the Spirit is love, joy, peace, patience, kindness, goodness, faithfulness, gentleness and self-control. Against such things there is no law. Those who belong to Christ Jesus have crucified the sinful nature with its passions and desires. Since we live by the Spirit, let us keep in step with the Spirit.

In her compassionate and practical book *The 20th-Century Plague: What will happen if we can't stop* AIDS? Dr Caroline Collier writes this:

42

The Bible teaches that God created us to live in a certain way, and both New and Old Testaments set out ideals for human behaviour as well as guidelines for committed Christian living. If an atheist says 'These ideals are irrelevant to me, because I do not believe in the existence of a Creator,' the Bible replies, 'You are wrong. Those ideals are inescapably relevant, because you are made in the image of the God you do not believe in.' In other words God created human beings, not Christians only. And his laws are framed for the well-being of the whole human race without distinction. The claim that some behaviour patterns lead to human health and happiness while others do not – simply because of the way people are made – surely merits a hearing from a generation which faces the global threat of AIDS. Perhaps this lay behind the embarrassment of an anonymous psychologist who cares for many AIDS patients, when he was asked by a journalist, 'If we had played by New Testament rules on sexual behaviour, would we have ever had an epidemic?' 'Of course not,' he replied, 'but, for God's sake, don't quote me on that!'

If we want a manifesto for Christian living we have only to read the Sermon on the Mount – those three chapters from 5 to 7 in Matthew's gospel that call us to a radically different way of living and loving. It starts with what are known as the Beatitudes, and tells us the way of blessedness – and of being in the truest sense blissfully happy. John Stott wrote a book on its message and called it *Christian Counter-Culture*. He says in the Preface:

I have wanted above all to let the Sermon speak, or better to let Christ speak it again, and speak it to the contemporary world. So I have sought to face with integrity the dilemmas which the Sermon raises for modern Christians, and not to dodge them. For Jesus did not give us an academic treatise calculated merely to stimulate the mind. I believe he meant his Sermon on the Mount to be obeyed. Indeed, if the church realistically accepted his standards and values as here set forth, and lived by them, it would be the alternative society he always intended it to be, and would offer to the world an authentic Christian counter-culture.

Back in the Old Testament the prophet Isaiah tells of the sort of society God wants his people to set up. The will of God with regard to social justice is spelt out so plainly that anyone can understand it, and God promises that when we do what he wants then our light will shine like the dawning of the sun:

> Is not this the fast that I choose:
>   to loose the bonds of wickedness,
>   to undo the thongs of the yoke,

Isaiah 58:6–11
RSV

43

to let the oppressed go free,
and to break every yoke?
Is it not to share your bread with the hungry,
and bring the homeless poor into your house;
when you see the naked, to cover him,
and not to hide yourself from your own flesh?
Then shall your light break forth like the dawn,
and your healing shall spring up speedily;
your righteousness shall go before you,
the glory of the Lord shall be your rear guard.
Then you shall call, and the Lord will answer;
you shall cry, and he will say,
Here I am.

If you take away from the midst of you the yoke,
the pointing of the finger, and speaking wickedness,
if you pour yourself out for the hungry
and satisfy the desire of the afflicted,
then shall your light rise in the darkness
and your gloom be as the noonday.
And the Lord will guide you continually,
and satisfy your desire with good things,
and make your bones strong;
and you shall be like a watered garden,
like a spring of water,
whose waters fail not.

Group material, prayers and meditation for chapter 5:
BEING CHRIST IN THE WORLD

1. Read out Romans 12:1–2 and 3–21 and then spend some time reflecting in silence on what Paul writes.
2. Ask each member of the group to share one thing that has struck them either in the Bible passage or in this chapter. Discuss these things with one another. How can we overcome evil with good?
3. Read out Teresa of Avila's words and talk about them.
4. Read out Isaiah 58:1–11.
5. Do you accept that the will of God is always the same, and that he still wants people to do what he told them to do through the prophet Isaiah? What could Christians do to change the world so that the will of God is done?

6. Go back to Romans 12:1–2. How can we change our own minds and prove what is the will of God?

A Meditation

Read out Teresa of Avila's words again, slowly, with pauses in between the phrases so that people can take them in and pray . . .
Then continue:
We are the body of Christ . . . Lord Jesus, that's what it says . . .
Help us to believe it . . . Help us to shine in the darkness . . . Help us to help the helpless . . .
Lord Jesus, you said, 'Whatever you wish that men would do to you, do so to them.'
If I was hungry I would want someone to feed me . . .
If I was without clothes I would want someone to clothe me . . .
If I was homeless I would want someone to give me a home . . . or to build me a home . . .
But I wouldn't want a do-gooding sort of charity, Lord. I'd want to be treated with respect, and given dignity – however hopeless I seemed – however helpless I seemed.
I'd want hope instead of hopelessness . . .
I'd want to be given a new start . . . and a new strength . . . I'd want real justice . . .
I'd want real love . . .
Lord Jesus, we call you Lord. Help us to love our neighbour as we love ourself.

A Prayer of Lord Shaftesbury – 'Father of the Forsaken'

O God, the father of the forsaken, the help of the weak, the supplier of the needy; you teach us that love towards the race of man is the bond of perfectness, and the imitation of your blessed self. Open and touch our hearts that we may see and do, both for this world and that which is to come, the things that belong to our peace. Strengthen us in the work we have undertaken; give us wisdom, perseverance, faith, and zeal, and in your own time and according to your pleasure prosper the issue; for the love of your Son Jesus Christ.

A Prayer of Alan Paton – 'The Work of Peace'

Give us courage, O Lord, to stand up and be counted,
to stand up for those who cannot stand up for themselves,

to stand up for ourselves when it is needful for us to do so.
Let us fear nothing more than we fear you.
Let us love nothing more than we love you,
for thus we shall fear nothing also.
Let us have no other God before you,
whether nation or party or state or church.
Let us seek no other peace but the peace which is yours,
and make us its instruments,
opening our eyes and our ears and our hearts,
so that we should know always what work of peace we may do for you.

After a short time of silence ask people to pray their own prayers aloud.

Finish by praying the Lord's Prayer together.

6. The Last Things

A woman known to a friend of mine began her will by writing, 'If anything should ever happen to me . . .'! Unfortunately, but not surprisingly, something *did* happen – and by the time her hopeful impossibility had been read out in public she was dead. She hadn't quite managed to come to terms with the fact that the death rate of the world's population at the moment is 100 per cent.

In the western world death is something that we hide behind the closed doors of a refrigerator so that we never (or almost never) see the decomposition and liquefaction of a dead body. We manage (or almost manage) not to see the reality of death. Other generations saw it much more plainly.

Holy Dying

In 1650 Jeremy Taylor wrote *Holy Living* and followed it up the next year with *Holy Dying*. They were printed together, and it has been said that no book other than the Bible and the Book of Common Prayer has had a more profound effect on English spirituality. It set John Wesley off on the journey that led to his conversion and for John Keble it was an epoch in his religious life.

The first chapter is 'A General Preparation towards a Holy and Blessed Death, by Way of Consideration' and it has in it, amongst other things, a 'Consideration of the vanity and shortness of man's life' and 'Rules and spiritual arts of lengthening our days, and to take off the objection of a short life.' Men and women come into the world 'like morning mushrooms, soon thrusting up their heads into the air, and conversing with their kindred of the same production, and as soon they turn into dust and forgetfulness.'

The rest of the book covers every possible aspect of dying, and there are rules, remedies and analyses together with various suitable prayers and acts of contrition.

We may smile to ourselves and think 'how depressing'. But it can be quite the opposite, and our own generation's refusal to look at death may be one of the chief reasons for our widespread depression and apathy. The old condition known as *accidie* was very like depression, and one of its remedies, strangely, was actually to think about death in general and our own death in particular.

The denial of death

The psychiatrist Franz Perls said that we are afraid to live because we are afraid to die. Ernest Becker won the Pulitzer Prize for 1974 with his book *The Denial of Death*: 'The idea of death, the fear of it, haunts the human animal like nothing else; it is a mainspring of human activity designed largely to avoid the fatality of death, to overcome it by denying in some way that it is the final destiny for man.'

Leonard Bernstein in his Harvard lectures on music through the centuries said that twentieth-century music is full of the sound of death, insisting that we listen to it in one way if we won't listen to it in another – because in our century death is the one thing that we refuse to speak about.

One day we shall all have to walk into the valley of the shadow of death. But it will make all the difference in the world if we know that the Lord who conquered death is our shepherd. It is gloriously possible to walk through that valley of deep darkness hand-in-hand with the one who called himself the light of the world.

'I will see God'

Hundreds of years before Jesus Christ was born Job had cried out in faith that one day he would experience life after the death and dissolution of his body: 'I know that my Redeemer lives, and that in the end he will stand upon the earth. And after my skin has been destroyed, yet in [or 'apart from'] my flesh I will see God; I myself will see him with my own eyes – I, and not another. How my heart yearns within me!' (Job 19:25–27 NIV).

Some of the Jews had started to believe in the resurrection of the dead later on in their history. But the rest of the ancient world was without hope; for them, death was the end. Into that desolation the Christian hope of eternal life shone like a light in the darkness. A Christian had a new relationship with the living God and Father of our Lord Jesus Christ, and because of the resurrection she or he had a new and living hope. The body would die, but it would be raised up to an endless life, imperishable and incorruptible.

Blessed be the God and Father of our Lord Jesus Christ! By his great mercy we have been born anew to a living hope through the resurrection of Jesus Christ from the dead, and to an inheritance which is imperishable, undefiled, and unfading, kept in heaven for you, who by God's power are guarded through faith for a salvation ready to be revealed in the last time.

1 Peter 1:3–5 RSV

Death is the friend

When David Watson the evangelist was dying of cancer at the age of 51, he said with utter confidence: 'Death is the friend who opens the door.' For the apostle Paul, writing to the church in

Philippi that he had founded and that he loved very deeply, death was gain:

Philippians
1:21–24 RSV To me to live is Christ, and to die is gain. If it is to be life in the flesh, that means fruitful labour for me. Yet which I shall choose I cannot tell. I am hard pressed between the two. My desire is to depart and be with Christ, for that is far better. But to remain in the flesh is more necessary on your account.

The New Testament says that Christians will see their Lord on the other side of the door of death. It says that Christ will come for them in the moment of their dying, and it says that when they see him they will somehow be like him.

When Jesus told his disciples about his impending death and the fact that he was going to the Father, they were troubled. But he told them not to be:

John 14:1–3
RSV Let not your hearts be troubled; believe in God, believe also in me. In my Father's house are many rooms; if it were not so, would I have told you that I go to prepare a place for you? And when I go and prepare a place for you, I will come again and will take you to myself, that where I am you may be also.

And in his first letter, John says this:

1 John 3:2–3
RSV Beloved, we are God's children now; it does not yet appear what we shall be, but we know that when he appears we shall be like him, for we shall see him as he is. And every one who thus hopes in him purifies himself as he is pure.

The vision of God

Right from the very beginning Christians have spoken and dreamed of the 'beatific vision', which is the direct knowledge of God enjoyed by the blessed in heaven. In the vision of heaven which John saw when he was in exile on the Isle of Patmos he says:

Revelation
21:1–8 RSV Then I saw a new heaven and a new earth; for the first heaven and the first earth had passed away, and the sea was no more. And I saw the holy city, new Jerusalem, coming down out of heaven from God,

prepared as a bride adorned for her husband; and I heard a loud voice from the throne saying, 'Behold, the dwelling of God is with men. He will dwell with them, and they shall be his people, and God himself will be with them; he will wipe away every tear from their eyes, and death shall be no more, neither shall there be mourning nor crying nor pain any more, for the former things have passed away.' And he who sat upon the throne said, 'Behold, I make all things new.' Also he said, 'Write this, for these words are trustworthy and true.' And he said to me, 'It is done! I am the Alpha and the Omega, the beginning and the end. To the thirsty I will give from the fountain of the water of life without payment. He who conquers shall have this heritage, and I will be his God and he shall be my son. But as for the cowardly, the faithless, the polluted, as for murderers, fornicators, sorcerers, idolaters, and all liars, their lot shall be in the lake that burns with fire and sulphur, which is the second death.

The darkest teaching Jesus ever gave

That last part of John's vision is a vision of hell, and hell is the darkest teaching Jesus ever gave. But we always have to look at it in the light of the love of God, and of Christ's lament over Jerusalem: 'O Jerusalem, Jerusalem, killing the prophets and stoning those who are sent to you! How often would I have gathered your children together as a hen gathers her brood under her wings, and you would not!' (Luke 13:34 RSV).

The love of God longs for us and yearns for us, but just as we can refuse and reject a human lover so we can refuse the divine lover – and refuse to accept the forgiveness of our sins which he offers to us.

Jesus warned people of the awful possibility of being 'thrown into hell, where their worm does not die and the fire is not quenched' (Mark 9:48 RSV). That word for hell is Gehenna, which was the name given by the people of Jerusalem to the great rubbish tip outside their city, where they threw away what was no longer any use, and where maggots crawled and fire burst out all the time on the decaying matter. But what we finally have to throw away can be something that we have very greatly loved.

We seem to have taken our pictures of hell more from Dante's *Inferno* and Michelangelo's 'Last Judgement' than from the

51

Bible. So we see it as a sort of demonic barbecue, where the devil eternally prods with his pitchfork the lost souls suspended over everlasting flames. Or we see it as a sort of vast lost property office, but with lost souls instead of lost umbrellas on the racks. And because we rightly find that unacceptable we often reject the doctrine of hell altogether.

Yet Jesus taught it, even in the Sermon on the Mount:

Matthew 7:13
RSV
Enter by the narrow gate; for the gate is wide and the way is easy that leads to destruction, and those who enter by it are many. For the gate is narrow and the way is hard that leads to life, and those who find it are few.

In John's gospel Jesus says that one day, when he judges the world, all the dead will hear his voice: 'Those who have *done good* will rise to live, and those who have done evil will rise to be condemned' (John 5:29 NIV).

Justified

A Christian does good just as a fig tree (not a thistle plant) bears figs. Martin Luther didn't like the epistle of James at all. He called it 'a right strawy Epistle', because it seemed to undercut the great and glorious doctrine of justification through faith and faith alone. But it doesn't. It simply shows how we behave when we *are* justified.

William Barclay explains what the word 'justification' means. It is a metaphor which comes from the law courts.

Let us remind ourselves again, the whole problem is, How can a man enter into a right relationship with God? This metaphor thinks of man on trial before God. Now the Greek word which is translated to *justify* is *diakioun*. All Greek verbs which end in *-oun* mean, not to *make* someone something, but to *treat*, to *reckon*, to *account* someone as something. If a man appears before a judge and that man *is* innocent, then to treat him as innocent is to *acquit* him (William Barclay, *Romans*).

But when we stand before God we are not innocent. We are guilty. All of us have sinned, and all of us fall short of the glory of

52

God. But the good news is that God still loves us and that Christ died for us. We are justified through faith if we simply believe that and put our trust in it.

For God so loved the world that he gave his only Son, that whoever believes in him should not perish but have eternal life. For God sent the Son into the world, not to condemn the world, but that the world might be saved through him. He who believes in him is not condemned; he who does not believe is condemned already, because he has not believed in the name of the only Son of God. And this is the judgment, that the light has come into the world, and men loved darkness rather than light, because their deeds were evil.

John 3:16–19 RSV

One of the simplest and the best descriptions ever written of how to be justified 'through faith alone' is Augustus Toplady's well known and much loved hymn:

> Rock of ages, cleft for me,
> Let me hide myself in Thee.
> Let the water and the blood,
> From Thy riven side which flowed,
> Be of sin the double cure:
> Cleanse me from its guilt and power.
>
> Not the labour of my hands
> Can fulfil Thy law's demands;
> Could my zeal no respite know,
> Could my tears for ever flow,
> All for sin could not atone:
> Thou must save, and Thou alone.
>
> Nothing in my hand I bring,
> Simply to Thy cross I cling;
> Naked, come to Thee for dress;
> Helpless, look to Thee for grace;
> Foul, I to the fountain fly;
> Wash me, Saviour, or I die.
>
> While I draw this fleeting breath,
> When my eyelids close in death,
> When I soar through tracts unknown,
> See Thee on Thy judgement throne;
> Rock of ages, cleft for me,
> Let me hide myself in Thee.

Once we are justified by faith it will show in our actions.

James 2:14–17
NIV What good is it, my brothers, if a man claims to have faith but has no deeds? Can such faith save him? Suppose a brother or sister is without clothes and daily food. If one of you says to him, 'Go, I wish you well, keep warm and well fed', but does nothing about his physical needs, what good is it? In the same way, faith by itself, if it is not accompanied by action, is dead.

Jesus our Judge

Jesus told us that one day we would be judged by our actions, and that he would be the judge.

Matthew
25:31–46 NIV When the Son of Man comes in his glory, and all the angels with him, he will sit on his throne in heavenly glory. All the nations will be gathered before him, and he will separate the people one from another as a shepherd separates the sheep from the goats. He will put the sheep on his right and the goats on his left.

Then the King will say to those on his right, 'Come, you who are blessed by my Father; take your inheritance, the kingdom prepared for you since the creation of the world. For I was hungry and you gave me something to eat, I was thirsty and you gave me something to drink, I was a stranger and you invited me in, I needed clothes and you clothed me, I was sick and you looked after me, I was in prison and you came to visit me.

Then the righteous will answer him, 'Lord, when did we see you hungry and feed you, or thirsty and give you something to drink? When did we see you a stranger and invite you in, or needing clothes and clothe you? When did we see you sick or in prison and go to visit you?

The King will reply, 'I tell you the truth, whatever you did for one of the least of these brothers of mine, you did it for me.'

Then he will say to those on his left, 'Depart from me, you who are cursed, into the eternal fire prepared for the devil and his angels. For I was hungry and you gave me nothing to eat, I was thirsty and you gave me nothing to drink, I was a stranger and you did not invite me in, I needed clothes and you did not clothe me, I was sick and in prison and you did not look after me.'

They also will answer, 'Lord, when did we see you hungry or thirsty or a stranger or needing clothes or sick or in prison, and did not help you?

He will reply, 'I tell you the truth, whatever you did not do for one of the least of these, you did not do for me.'

Then they will go away to eternal punishment, but the righteous to eternal life.

If we are the children of God, who is utterly good, and who is love, then we shall do good and loving things to other people. We don't become the children of God through what we do. But if we are God's children then the nature of God in us will shine out through what we do. Jesus said, 'Let your light so shine before men, that they may see your good works and give glory to your Father who is in heaven' (Matthew 5:16 RSV).

Hell

But what if we don't choose to come to God and be forgiven and given new life as a child of God? Then it isn't and cannot be that the God who loves each one of us punishes us and sends us to hell out of spite. It is simply that he has nothing else to give but himself. Hell is separation from God, and he gives us what we want. If we don't want him, and if we refuse to receive him, then even he is helpless.

We do not like the idea of a helpless God. But Christianity shows us a God who is helpless as a baby in a manger, helpless as a man nailed to a cross. C. S. Lewis says, 'If we will not eat the only food which the universe provides then we must remain forever hungry.' That food is God himself; the life of God, offering love and forgiveness to the whole world through the death of Christ.

If we refuse it, then we shall not have eternal life: 'You refuse to come to me that you might have life,' Jesus said to some people; and the opposite of life is death.

The New Testament says that there will be a second death, after the death of our bodies and following the judgement of Christ. What is eternal about the punishment is that its consequences last for ever. The human being who could have been a son or daughter of God for all eternity is finally dead, cut off for ever from the God of love who is the source of all life.

A glory beyond imagining

But what about those of us who are the sons and daughters of God now, forgiven sinners through the death of Christ, and with the Spirit of Christ living within our hearts? We have a glory beyond imagining to look forward to. John's vision of the city of God gives us a glimpse of it:

Revelation 22:1–5 RSV

Then he showed me the river of the water of life, bright as crystal, flowing from the throne of God and of the Lamb through the middle of the street of the city; also, on either side of the river, the tree of life with its twelve kinds of fruit, yielding its fruit each month; and the leaves of the tree were for the healing of the nations. There shall no more be anything accursed, but the throne of God and of the Lamb shall be in it, and his servants shall worship him; they shall see his face, and his name shall be on their foreheads. And night shall be no more; they need no light of lamp or sun, for the Lord God will be their light, and they shall reign for ever and ever.

C. S. Lewis described the same future hope in the simple words of a children's story, *The Last Battle*:

'There *was* a real railway accident,' said Aslan softly. 'Your father and mother and all of you are – as you used to call it in the Shadowlands – dead. The term is over: the holidays have begun. The dream is ended: this is the morning.'

And as He spoke He no longer looked to them like a lion; but the things that began to happen after that were so great and beautiful that I cannot write them. And for us this is the end of all the stories, and we can most truly say that they all lived happily ever after. But for them it was only the beginning of the real story. All their life in this world and all their adventures in Narnia had only been the cover and the title page: now at last they were beginning Chapter One of the Great Story, which no one on earth has read: which goes on for ever: in which every chapter is better than the one before.

Group material, meditation and prayers for chapter 6:
THE LAST THINGS

1. Read out Matthew 25:34–46. Talk about it. Do you believe that one day we are going to be judged? If not – why not?!

2. Read out John 14:1–3 and 1 John 3:2–3. Do you believe that Christians are God's children now, and that at the moment of our death Christ will come for us?

3. Read out Revelation 21:1–5. Discuss the things that John sees in his vision. Remember that visions are not meant to be taken literally. They are packed with signs and symbols that we have to unpack – and they can affect us and speak to us in the deepest places of our heart and mind. Talk about hell and about heaven.

Prayers and Meditation

Start with a time of silence.
Ask people to pray their own prayers out loud.

Then read out Revelation 22:1–5, very slowly, so that people can take it in and God can speak to them.

Read out the extract from *The Last Battle*.

Finish with this blessing, which Martin Luther King spoke to his church in Montgomery when he left them to devote his time to political action:

And now unto him who is able to keep us from falling and lift us from the dark valley of despair to the bright mountain of hope, from the midnight of desperation to the daybreak of joy; to him be power and authority, for ever and ever.   Amen

PART TWO

PART TWO

7. Our Father

Just like us, Jesus' first disciples needed some help with their praying. So they asked Jesus to give it to them. 'Lord, teach us to pray . . .' The words he taught them transformed their theology and their understanding of God: 'When you pray, this is what to say: '*Father . . .*'

> Father, hallowed be thy name.
> Thy kingdom come.
> Give us each day our daily bread;
> and forgive us our sins,
> for we ourselves forgive everyone
> who is indebted to us;
> and lead us not into temptation.

Luke 11:2–4
RSV

Unless he had told them to, they would never have dared to say it. The Jew was in such awe of God that he would not even pronounce his name, YHWH, out loud, and he only ever wrote down the consonants and left out the vowels. God had told it to Moses, and it meant either I AM WHO (or WHAT) I AM, or I WILL BE WHAT I WILL BE (Exodus 3:14). The self-existent one, whose name was holy. The One to whom everything that is owes its existence – the stars in the sky, millions of light years away from our little planet earth; all the living things on the earth: blackbirds and baby seals, tigers and humming birds, and you and me and the disciples of Jesus.

Those Jews knew far less than we do about the vastness of the universe. But still they knew it was far bigger than they were, and when they gazed up into the night sky they were aware of the greatness of God and their own smallness:

Psalm 8:1, 3–4
NIV

> O Lord, our Lord,
>   how majestic is your name in all the earth! . . .
> When I consider your heavens,
>   the work of your fingers,
> the moon and the stars,
>   which you have set in place,
> what is man that you are mindful of him,
>   the son of man that you care for him?

The Jews believed it was a risky business to get too close to God. The proper channels of communication were through priests and sacrifices, and although they worshipped and adored it was mostly from a safe distance. The God with the name they never spoke was utterly holy – and now Jesus was telling them to call that God Father.

The possibility was there in the Old Testament, but they had never dared to do it. In the book of Hosea they had heard God speaking through the prophet, and he showed them a father's heart yearning after a son who had gone wrong and remembering how he helped the baby son that he loved to take his first, wobbling steps:

Hosea 11:1–4
NJB

> When Israel was a child I loved him,
> and I called my son out of Egypt.
> But the more I called,
>   the further they went away from me;
> they offered sacrifice to Baal
> and burnt incense to idols.
> I myself taught Ephraim to walk,
> I myself took them by the arm,
> but they did not know
>   that I was the one caring for them,
> that I was leading them with human ties,

with leading-strings of love,
that, with them, I was like someone
    lifting an infant to his cheek,
and that I bent down to feed him.

'When you pray, say, "Father" . . .' That is what Jesus said two thousand years ago in a different land with a different culture. But it wasn't completely different. There are enough examples in scripture to show us that fathers still loved their children and cared very deeply about what happened to them. Those words from Hosea are one example, and the story of the Prodigal Son, or the Waiting Father, is another, perhaps the most loved of all the stories that Jesus told to show us what the Father is like (see pages 5–6).

In the Old Testament God comforted his people better than any mother.

Isaiah
49:13–16 NIV

Shout for joy, O heavens;
    rejoice, O earth;
    burst into song, O mountains!
For the Lord comforts his people
    and will have compassion on his afflicted ones.

But Zion said, 'The Lord has forsaken me,
    the Lord has forgotten me.'

'Can a mother forget the baby at her breast
    and have no compassion on the child she has borne?
Though she may forget,
    I will not forget you!
See, I have engraved you on the palms of my hands;
    your walls are ever before me.'

As a mother comforts her child,
    so will I comfort you.

Isaiah 66:13 NIV

Good and bad fathers

When we realize that we are praying to a loving, heavenly Father it unlocks within us all the things that we feel we can talk to him about. But some people's experience of their own fathers is so bad that it distorts their relationship with God. Then they need to experience the inner healing that can be known through the ministry of the Christian church.

Charlie, a friend of Gavin's, is the son of a great missionary hero. But the father drove the whole family, as well as himself, so hard in pursuit of his calling that Charlie still cannot manage to say the words of the General Thanksgiving to God the Father: 'I thank you for my creation, preservation and for all the blessings of this life.' Imprinted on Charlie's memory is the appalling severity of the demands his father made on him – still unhealed and unforgiven.

Gavin does not think it is any coincidence that his own father had two sons who are both Christians and in the Christian ministry. He was a marvellous father and made it easy for them to believe in a loving, fatherly God.

We can make it easier for our children to believe, not just through what we try to teach them in our family prayers, but through their experiencing something of the divine nature in us, as we express fatherhood and motherhood to them.

Pray about everything

The fact that we are praying to a loving heavenly father unlocks both what we should pray about (not just for: that is only a fraction of what prayer is about) and how we should pray. Gavin likes his (grown-up) children to talk to him about everything that is happening to them. He liked them to do it when they were small, and he still likes it now they are grown up. It isn't that he is inquisitive: just enormously interested, because of the relationship.

In *Clinical Theology* Dr Frank Lake wrote about the importance of talking to God totally honestly about everything. He was thinking about a depressed person who has 'stopped praying because he cannot, or feels he cannot, turn either the depravities of rage and lust, or the deprivations of faithlessness, anxiety and emptiness into prayer.' But the sort of praying he is talking about is what we should all be doing.

He goes on to say:

Prayer as communication with God cannot be re-established unless he can bring his complaints, objections, demands, accusations, resentments, doubts and disbeliefs out of hiding, and into conversation with the pastor and with God . . . The task of clinical pastoral care is to evoke the truth in the inward parts, however scandalous it may be, so as to bring the total actual content of the personality and its roots into the conversation with God – which is prayer.

That sort of praying is just as essential for us as for someone who is in a depression – and if we really talk to God about everything we are probably less likely to get depressed. God knows about everything that is happening to us anyway. But the conversation about it, which is part of what prayer is, affects and transforms both us and whatever is happening. And if we can't talk about it comfortably to God then it probably oughtn't to be happening anyway.

The wrong sort of praying

There are some prayers which God cannot answer. Or at least, the answer to them will probably be 'No!' Immediately after the prayer to the Father in Luke 11, which we call the Lord's Prayer, Jesus talks about the utter impossibility of a human father giving a snake to the son who has asked him for a fish. But what if the son had asked for a snake? It may be that some of the things we cry for to our heavenly Father would be as dangerous to us as a snake.

Sometimes, if we cry loud enough, we get what we want and learn from the mistake of our insisting. Psalm 106 looks back to the story of the Israelites in the wilderness crying out for meat and says, 'He gave them what they asked' [a flock of quails flew down] 'but sent a wasting disease among them.' When they ate the quails and satisfied their craving for meat it had a totally unexpected effect. Instead of getting fatter they got thinner. The Authorized Version translates it more poetically and gives us the deeper meaning: 'He gave them their request, but sent leanness into their soul.'

Margaret had a deep desire (craving would describe it better) to marry a clergyman. Not a particular clergyman – any clergyman! Like the song in *Joseph and the Technicolour Dreamcoat*, 'Any dream will do'! She managed to do it (poor Margaret, and poor man), and ended up with a desperately unhappy marriage and a nervous breakdown.

The fact that we are praying to our heavenly Father also answers the question of how we should pray. Can we possibly imagine going to talk to our own father and trying to invent a special form of English in which to speak to him as opposed to anyone else? It is one thing to make our formal liturgies as beautiful as possible so far as the language goes – and even they still need to be in the ordinary day-to-day speech of the 1990s. It would be very odd to speak either to our earthly or our heavenly father in old-fashioned, out-of-date language and forms of address. People say they feel that it is more reverent but it can be less real and somehow make the relationship more distant. If your child wants to take a packed lunch to school, do you make her say, 'I beseech thee that thou

YEAH, VERILY THOU HAST GRANTED MY EARNEST REQUEST, BUT I AM SURELY VEXED AS COKE DOTH NOW COST 35p. A CAN ......!!

wilt do me up a cheese and tomato roll and that thou wilt deign to grant me 30p for a can of coke'?

That is not to say that when people talk to God in the language of another age, their relationship with God may not be far richer than the young man who said brashly, 'The Almighty is my greatest pal!' But we don't know. Only God knows what goes on in other people's hearts. If we really want to know what goes on in our own hearts, we can ask God to show us. Are we distancing ourselves from God and holding him at arm's length through the formality of our language? Or are we failing to see the glory and the holiness of God when we addrress him slangily?

'Not yet'

But whatever language we use, and however we pray, the answer to our prayers of petition is not always 'Yes'.

Any parent knows that 'now' may not be the right time to give a new bike to one of our children. She might need to get a bit older before she is ready for it. Or perhaps she wants our permission to spend all her money on a particular bike – and we already have it in mind to give her a better quality one on Christmas morning.

Sometimes, like a human parent, God says a straight 'No'. Sometimes the answer is 'Not yet'.

But all our prayer begins where Jesus told us to begin. 'When you pray, say, "Father . . ." '

Group material, prayers and meditations for chapter 7:
OUR FATHER

1. Read the Bible passages aloud, and keep silent for at least a minute or two (time it if you are leading) after each one to reflect on it.
2. In just one sentence, share with the rest of the group what you think of when you think of 'father' in human terms. Perhaps write them on a board.

3. Think of one or two sad, true stories of how fathers have treated their children.

4. Jesus describes God as a loving Father. Do you think of him like that? If not, how can you change your thinking and your belief? There are many people whose fathers have been cruel to them or subjected them to sexual and other abuse when they were children. How can those people discover what God is really like?

5. Discuss points that have particularly struck you in the chapter and in the Bible readings.

6. How honest are you in your prayers? Do you pray about everything? Read out the passage from Frank Lake (page 65). Are you open with God about everything in your life, or do you find it difficult. Will you dare to be more open, more trusting?

Then have a time of silence.
Ask people to pray their own prayers aloud, if they would like to.

Then perhaps use this meditation:

Lord Jesus Christ, you taught us to call God Father . . . to pray to him as Father . . . Give us your Spirit now, to teach us more about the Father . . . your Father . . . our Father . . .

Help each of us now to think of ourself as a prodigal son . . . a prodigal daughter . . . taking from the Father everything that he'll give us . . . help us to think of the things we have . . . the things we possess . . . somewhere to live, if we're fortunate . . . food to eat . . . friends . . . help us to imagine enjoying those things, those people, away from the Father's presence . . . in a far country . . .

Help us to think of the Father . . . waiting . . . longing for us . . . yearning for us . . . Help us to see things from his point of view . . . to feel the pain of the Father's heart . . . aching . . .

Help us to imagine ourselves going home . . . back to the Father's presence . . . to the Father's love . . . that never stopped loving us . . .

'Let's have a feast and celebrate. For this son of mine was dead and is alive again, he was lost and is found . . . This daughter of mine was dead and is alive again, she was lost and is found . . .

Help us now, in the Father's presence, to speak to him in the silence of our hearts . . . about the things that are in our hearts . . . help us to listen to what he says to us . . .

Spend from three to five minutes in silence . . . (Whoever is reading the meditation should say in advance that this is what is going to happen, and that it will be brought to an end with a prayer.)

A Prayer of St Paul

Let us pray for ourselves what Paul prayed for the Ephesians:

'I kneel before the Father, from whom his whole family in heaven and on earth derives its name. I pray that out of his glorious riches he may strengthen you with power through his Spirit in your inner being, so that Christ may dwell in your hearts through faith. And I pray that you, being rooted and established in love, may have power, together with all the saints, to grasp how wide and long and high and deep is the love of Christ, and to know this love that surpasses knowledge – that you may be filled to the measure of all the fulness of God.'

Ephesians 3:14–19 NIV

Say together: 'Our Father . . .'

8. Hallowed be Your Name

If we asked a hundred school children what the word 'hallowed' means we would probably get a hundred different answers, and probably most of them would be wrong. It isn't a word that we use in ordinary conversation – only when we say the Lord's Prayer.

Perhaps the way to a deeper understanding of it is through Hallowe'en, which was essentially a Christian festival, but has now utterly wrong associations. Hallowe'en is short for All Hallows Even, the evening before All Hallows Day – the feast in the Christian church that now we call All Saints Day. The saints are the holy ones, and the word 'hallow' simply means holy or consecrated. To hallow a place or a person means 'to make holy', or 'to set apart for holy use', or 'to respect greatly and to venerate'. When we hallow something we are saying that it is sacred.

The holiness of God

Sacredness and holiness have to do with God, because God is holy. When human beings become aware of the presence of God they fall on their faces and worship. That is what happened to Isaiah in his vision of God:

In the year that King Uzziah died, I saw the Lord seated on a throne, high and exalted, and the train of his robe filled the temple. Above him were seraphs, each with six wings: With two wings they covered their faces, with two they covered their feet, and with two they were flying. And they were calling to one another:

Isaiah 6:1–8 NIV

> 'Holy, holy, holy is the Lord Almighty,
> the whole earth is full of his glory.'

At the sound of their voices the doorposts and thresholds shook and the temple was filled with smoke.
'Woe to me!' I cried. 'I am ruined! For I am a man of unclean lips, and I live among a people of unclean lips, and my eyes have seen the King, the Lord Almighty.'
Then one of the seraphs flew to me with a live coal in his hand, which he had taken with tongs from the altar. With it he touched my mouth and said, 'See, this has touched your lips: your guilt is taken away and your sin atoned for.'
Then I heard the voice of the Lord saying, 'Whom shall I send? And who will go for us?'
And I said, 'Here am I. Send me!'

Our God is a holy God. His nature is holy and his name is holy. Nothing will ever change that. So what are we praying when we pray, 'Hallowed be your name?'

We are not simply asking that people should keep the third of the Ten Commandments, that 'You shall not take the name of the Lord your God in vain.' Even so, it is worth asking ourselves what we feel when we hear people taking the name of God in vain and using 'God' and 'Christ' as swear words. When Gavin was in the supermarket recently he found himself considerably shaken and quite shocked when a small boy pointed at something on the shelf and said to his mother: 'Oh God, look at that!'

A holy world

Before we can pray 'Hallowed be your name', we need to be aware of the way things are in the world where it isn't hallowed.

71

One of the things that is missing in our world today is a sense of reverence. It is missing in religion and it is missing in sex. We probably talk about sex more than any generation has ever talked about it, but we don't understand it because we don't see the sacredness of it. Even in a Christian bookshop people will sometimes smirk at a title like *The Sanctity of Sex*, and when they do it betrays a deep and tragic failure in understanding.

Most of us love those superb animal programmes that David Attenborough and other people present on television, and when I watch them I find myself marvelling and worshipping God for creating such a wonderful world. But when I see two great elephants coming together to make a baby elephant I switch off or look away. It isn't that I find it in any sense unpleasant. Quite the reverse. Rather that their coupling is so beautiful and sacred that it should be private.

The love story that is at the heart of the Bible ought to be compulsory reading for all Christians. The songs of human love in the Song of Songs show us something of the love of God, and Jews and Christians have always seen that book as an allegory of the relationship between God and his beloved people.

The Jewish *Mishnah* says that 'all the Writings are holy, but the Song of Songs is the Holy of Holies' (the innermost place in the Jewish temple where the presence of God dwelt). And the Jews said that the presence of God, the *shekinah* glory, shone over a husband and wife when they were in their marriage bed.

Song of Songs 1:12–17 RSV

While the king was on his couch,
  my nard gave forth its fragrance.
My beloved is to me a bag of myrrh,
  that lies between my breasts.
My beloved is to me a cluster of henna blossoms
  in the vineyards of Engedi.

Behold, you are beautiful, my love;
  behold you are beautiful;
  your eyes are doves.
Behold, you are beautiful, my beloved,
  truly lovely.

Our couch is green;
   the beams of our house are cedar,
   our rafters are pine.

In the Song of Songs the man and the woman take great delight in each other – body as well as personality. For the Hebrew a person was body, soul and spirit, and if Christianity had stuck with its Jewishness we would never have torn apart those things which God has joined together.

The church has been affected by Greek thought, which 'separates the ideal from the actual, heaven from earth, time from eternity, body from soul, male from female, love from sex', and this separation has brought about in the West 'the promiscuous and permissive society that the rest of the world despises.' That is what A. F. Knight and Fridemann W. Golka wrote in their book on *The Song of Songs and Jonah: Revelation of God.*

It is not only in the area of sex that we miss out in our understanding of the holy and the sacred. Sometimes on television the camera will show us a close-up of a woman's face, weeping because her husband has been blown up by a terrorist's bomb. Gavin feels deeply that if we had a proper sense of respect, that sort of picture would never be taken, because her grief is a private thing that ought not to be probed into by a camera lens for all the world to look at.

If we could rediscover the sacred it would be a great benefit to us and to the world. In some ways the Green movement is beginning to do this, although some of that is really about survival – saying that if we are to survive, and if our children are to survive, then we must run our world more efficiently.

What Christians ought to do is to love the world that God made and be aware of the sacredness of it. In our technological, matter-of-fact age we need to realize that there is more to life than just being efficient. There are things that we can never assess in terms of whether they are efficient or effective. Things like beauty. We cannot look at a beautiful face and say exactly what it is that makes it beautiful. We cannot define beauty and we cannot define

THIS IS GOING TO HURT ME FAR MORE THAN IT IS GOING TO HURT YOU!

sacredness. But we know what they are and we know that we need them.

When the American Indians had to cut down a tree they used to speak to it and apologize. When my poplar trees had to be cut down I did the same thing. They grew at the end of my garden, and I loved them. I used to listen to their leaves rustling all through the summer, and in the winter I would look at their great branches silhouetted against the sky. And as I looked at them I always found myself worshipping the God who created them.

All things can make us aware of God. We can take an orange from the fruit bowl, peel it, and put the pieces in our mouth without thinking about it. But if sometimes we peel it carefully, and open it up and really look at it, we shall become aware that no one has ever seen before what we are seeing now. It has been growing in the sunlight and in the rain, and we are holding a holy thing in our hands. Then we can't just gobble it up. There is a holiness about the simple act of eating. If we go trampling through the world without seeing the holiness and the glory of it, then we are profoundly destitute human beings.

> Earth's crammed with heaven,
> And every common bush afire with God;
> But only he who sees takes off his shoes,
> The rest sit round it and pluck blackberries.
> (Elizabeth Barrett Browning, *Aurora Leigh*)

The world and all the things and the people in it are holy because they were made, and are being made, by a holy God. In that brilliant encounter which Jesus had with the Pharisees over whether or not they should pay taxes to Caesar, he tells them to go and get a coin. Then he asks them whose image is on it. 'Caesar's', they reply. So he tells them to give to Caesar what belongs to Caesar and to give to God what belongs to God – which is really saying, 'Give yourself and your heart to God, because you are made in the image and likeness of God. Just as the tax coin bears Caesar's image, so you bear God's.

Hallowed be your name

In one of the experimental Communion services in the Church of England the confession admitted to God that 'We have marred your image within us' – and to mar something means to detract from its perfection or wholeness: to spoil it. But we can still see something of the image and likeness of God in every human being – like a damaged portrait by a great painter.

Once we see the image and the glory we shall see every human being as sacred – even the worst of us. We shall delight in the fact that God-in-Christ is the great restorer of damaged images – and perhaps look with deeper understanding at the translation of Ephesians 2:10 which says that 'We are God's work of art.' And we shall pray with deeper passion that even the terrorist, the rapist, the pornographer and the child-abuser will hallow the name of God.

Our prayer is that they will know what the name and the nature of God is, and that God will shine in their hearts 'to give the light of the knowledge of the glory of God in the face of Jesus Christ.' Our task is to live in the light of the glory ourselves. To let the light shine on the whole of our life. On everything that we do and everything that we say. On all our relationships. Then we shall be doing on earth what is done in heaven.

Revelation 4:1–11 NIV

After this I looked, and there before me was a door standing open in heaven. And the voice I had first heard speaking to me like a trumpet said, 'Come up here, and I will show you what must take place after this.' At once I was in the spirit, and there before me was a throne in heaven with someone sitting on it. And the one who sat there had the appearance of jasper and carnelian. A rainbow, resembling an emerald, encircled the throne. Surrounding the throne were twenty-four other thrones, and seated on them were twenty-four elders. They were dressed in white and had crowns of gold on their heads. From the throne came flashes of lightning, rumblings and peals of thunder. Before the throne, seven lamps were blazing. These are the seven spirits of God. Also before the throne there was what looked like a sea of glass, clear as crystal.

In the centre, around the throne, were four living creatures, and they were covered with eyes, in front and behind. The first living creature was like a lion, the second was like an ox, the third had a face like a man, the fourth was like a flying eagle. Each of the four living creatures had six wings and was covered with eyes all around, even under his wings. Day and night they never stop saying:

> 'Holy, holy, holy
> is the Lord God Almighty,
> who was, and is, and is to come.'

Whenever the living creatures give glory, honour and thanks to him who sits on the throne and who lives for ever and ever, the twenty-four elders fall down before him who sits on the throne, and worship him who lives for ever and ever. They lay their crowns before the throne and say:

> 'You are worthy, our Lord and God,
>   to receive glory and honour and power,
> for you created all things,
>   and by your will they were created
>   and have their being.'

Meditation and prayers for chapter 8:
HALLOWED BE YOUR NAME

Start with a time of silence.
Then, perhaps, use this meditation. Read it out very slowly, with silence in between each phrase of it:

Father, hallowed be your name . . .
Your name is holy, and that means that you are holy . . .
Show us, each one of us here now, what it means to be holy . . .
Show us the beauty of holiness . . .
Show us how to be holy . . .
Show us how to hallow your name . . .
Jesus said, 'Give to Caesar what belongs to Caesar – give to God what belongs to God.' . . .
We belong to you – You created us in your image and your likeness . . .
Help each one of us to give ourself to you . . .
Help us to serve the world that you create and that you love . . .
Help us to pray with our whole heart: 'Hallowed be your name.'

A Prayer of George Appleton

    O God, I thank thee
    for all the creatures thou hast made,
    so perfect in their kind –
    great animals like the elephant and the rhinoceros,
    humorous animals like the camel and the monkey,
    friendly ones like the dog and the cat,
    working ones like the squirrel and the rabbit,
    majestic ones like the lion and the tiger,
    for birds with their songs.
    O Lord give us such love for thy creation
    that love may cast out fear,
    and all thy creatures see in man
    their priest and friend,
    through Jesus Christ our Lord.

Have another time of silence. Then:

1. Read the Bible passages aloud and spend at least a minute or two after each one to reflect on it.

2. Ask each person to share with the rest of the group (in one sentence) what the word 'holy' or 'hallowed' means to them.

3. Discuss the points that have particularly struck you in the chapter and in the Bible readings.

4. Are there any particular things in our society today that cut right across the prayer 'Hallowed be your name'? How could we pray for those situations and those people?

5. Finish with a time of prayer, either more silence or/and asking people to pray their own prayers aloud, if they would like to.

Say together: 'Our Father . . .'

9. *Your Kingdom Come, Your Will be Done*

The prayer 'Your will be done' was right at the heart of Jesus' life. He prayed it to the Father in the agony of Gethsemane when he faced his death on a cross: 'My Father, if it is not possible for this cup to be taken away unless I drink it, may your will be done.' 'Your will be done' is at the heart of the Lord's Prayer, and when we can pray it right from the bottom of our hearts then we are praying right.

But what does it mean to pray 'Your kingdom come'? The trouble with the idea of a kingdom is that it isn't a very contemporary image. Apart from Middle Eastern potentates, kings and queens don't have much power in the twentieth century. But in Jesus' day they did. A kingdom had a king who reigned over it and had authority over his subjects and decreed its laws.

For us in the twentieth century the idea of someone telling us what to do doesn't appeal at all. What we are interested in is freedom. We are wary of people having too much power, even the best of people. When someone gets a lot of power in their hands we remember uneasily Lord Acton's famous saying: 'Power tends to corrupt and absolute power corrupts absolutely.'

But the power of God is different from human power:

Revelation 4:11
NIV

> You are worthy, our Lord and God,
>   to receive glory and honour and power,
> for you created all things,
>   and by your will they were created
>   and have their being.

Free to choose

God doesn't use his power to *make* us do his will. Instead he gives us the freedom to choose. Either to pray 'Your kingdom come, your will be done', or not to pray it. God has created a universe in which we have choices.

Imagine a school head, who wants the pupils to grow up to be thoughtful, reasonably well-educated, compassionate human beings. So he sets up structures through which they can learn: how to read and write and add up; how to think (about all sorts of things as well as their lessons), and how to relate to other people.

To the extent that the pupils use the opportunities for learning that are there for them, they will grow. They will have done just what the head wants them to do. But if they spend their time breaking up the desks, writing on the walls, and beating up each other and their teachers, then they won't learn, they won't grow, and they won't have done what the head desires, or what is best for them. The head could make them do it by force, but it wouldn't be very successful. We cannot make someone learn if they don't want to (any more than we can make someone love us). We can exert pressure, but as soon as we take it off the person will revert to what she or he was.

The only way the head can get his will done and also allow the pupils their freedom is to try to persuade them that what they are being offered is for their own good, and that by rejecting the offer they are harming themselves.

The kingdom of God, in modern terms, could be said to be like that. God is the Head, and we are the pupils. The kingdom is what happens when the students do the will of the head.

Jesus the King

The kingdom of God is what happens when the will of God is done, and the kingdom is present when the King is present. What all the gospel writers say, in different ways, is that Jesus always did the will of God, and that the kingdom of God was therefore 'at hand' or 'had come upon them'.

The will of God is that there should be justice and true freedom. At the start of his ministry, after the temptation in the wilderness, 'Jesus returned to Galilee in the power of the Spirit, and news about him spread through the whole countryside. He taught in their synagogues, and everyone praised him' (Luke 4:14–15 NIV).

He went into the synagogue in Nazareth on the Sabbath and read to them from the scroll of the prophet Isaiah:

> The Spirit of the Lord is on me,
> because he has anointed me
> to preach good news to the poor.
> He has sent me to proclaim freedom for the prisoners
> and recovery of sight for the blind,
> to release the oppressed,
> to proclaim the year of the Lord's favour.

Luke 4:16–19
NIV

But the people in his home town soon stopped praising him. They didn't accept him, because his message was too tough. They were furious, and drove him out of the town. So the will of God wasn't done there, and the kingdom of God didn't come there.

The will of God

The will of God is always done in heaven. Jesus told us to pray 'Your will be done on earth as it is in heaven.' Heaven is where God lives, and because of that heaven can be in many places.

Isaiah 57:15 NIV

> For this is what the high and lofty One says –
>> he who lives for ever, whose name is holy,
> 'I live in a high and holy place,
>> but also with him who is contrite
>> and lowly in spirit,
> to revive the spirit of the lowly
>> and to revive the heart of the contrite.'

Those words come in the middle of God's passionate call through Isaiah to repentance and holiness. If the people will turn away from their wickedness and do the will of God, then God will come and live with them. But they must stop doing wrong and learn to do right:

Isaiah 1:10–11, 15–20 NIV

> Hear the word of the Lord,
>> you rulers of Sodom:
> listen to the law of our God,
>> you people of Gomorrah!
> 'The multitude of your sacrifices –
>> what are they to me?' says the Lord . . .
> 'When you spread out your hands in prayer,
>> I will hide my eyes from you;
> even if you offer many prayers,
>> I will not listen.
> Your hands are full of blood;
>> wash and make yourselves clean.
> Take your evil deeds
>> out of my sight!
> Stop doing wrong,
>> learn to do right!
> Seek justice,
>> encourage the oppressed.
> Defend the cause of the fatherless,
>> plead the cause of the widow.
>
> 'Come now, let us reason together,'
>> says the Lord.

'Though your sins are like scarlet,
   they shall be as white as snow;
though they are red as crimson,
   they shall be like wool.
If you are willing and obedient,
   you will eat the best from the land;
but if you resist and rebel,
   you will be devoured by the sword.'

That passage tells us what the will of God is. But we cannot do it in our own strength. The only way we shall ever do the will of the Father is to have the Spirit of his Son living in the heart of us: for God to live in us and for us to live in God, just as a branch lives in a tree. Jesus told his disciples the way of it:

John 15:1–5 NIV I am the true vine, and my Father is the gardener. He cuts off every branch in me that bears no fruit, while every branch that does bear fruit he trims clean so that it will be even more fruitful. You are already clean because of the word I have spoken to you. Remain in me, and I will remain in you. No branch can bear fruit by itself; it must remain in the vine. Neither can you bear fruit unless you remain in me. I am the vine; you are the branches. If a man remains in me and I in him, he will bear much fruit; apart from me you can do nothing.

'Here am I. Send me!'

When we pray 'Your kingdom come, your will be done', we are asking God to act and also offering ourselves to help in the action. When Isaiah saw the Lord in his holiness and heard what was needed, he said 'Here am I. Send me!'

When Nehemiah cried out to God to bring back the exiles to Jerusalem he was saying to God, 'You have told us what your will is – so now will you do it?' But he was willing for God to use him so that the will of God could be done. Nehemiah lived in a sinful society, and he identified himself with it in profound intercessory prayer:

Nehemiah 1:4–11 NIV When I heard these things [of the destruction of Jerusalem], I sat down and wept. For some days I mourned and fasted and prayed before the God of heaven. Then I said: 'O Lord, God of heaven, the great and awesome God, who keeps his covenant of love with those who love him and obey his commands, let your ear be attentive and your eyes open to hear the prayer your servant is praying before you day and night for your servants, the people of Israel. I confess the sins we Israelites, including myself and my father's house, have committed against you. We have acted very wickedly towards you. We have not obeyed the commands, decrees and laws you gave your servant Moses.

'Remember the instruction you gave your servant Moses, saying, "If you are unfaithful, I will scatter you among the nations, but if you return to me and obey my commands, then even if your exiled people are at the farthest horizon, I will gather them from there and bring them to the place I have chosen as a dwelling for my Name."

'They are your servants and your people, whom you redeemed by your great strength and your mighty hand. O Lord, let your ear be attentive to the prayer of this your servant and to the prayer of your servants who delight in revering your name. Give your servant success today by granting him favour in the presence of this man.'

I was cupbearer to the king.

As cupbearer to the king Nehemiah then put his life on the line. He went into the presence of the king to ask for what was necessary in order that the will of God could be done – and the king granted him his request.

'Your will be done'

It is no use praying for something that isn't the will of God. We may not always know what that will is, but we almost always know what it isn't.

Corrie ten Boom tells a story of how she wanted to smuggle something through the customs and started to pray, 'Lord, help me to get it through . . .' But the prayer fizzled out unsaid. She couldn't pray it, because she realized that it couldn't be the will of God to break this particular human law.

There may be human laws that we have to break, if we live in evil and unjust societies. If a corrupt government should take power in our nation and order to us persecute or kill a particular group of people in our midst, then we would have to disobey.

The persecution of the Jews and the horror of the gas chambers in Nazi Germany was never the will of God, and some Christians disobeyed the human laws. Some of them, like Dietrich Bonhoeffer, died for their disobedience.

Corrie ten Boom herself, and her sister Betsy, were imprisoned in the terrible Ravensbruck prison camp because during the German occupation of Holland they and their mother and father sheltered Jews in their house. To protect a Jew was the will of God. To smuggle a watch through the customs, however, wasn't. So she couldn't pray for it.

1. Read the Bible passages (except Nehemiah) aloud and spend some time reflecting on them in silence.
2. Discuss a few points that have particularly struck you in the Bible readings and in the chapter itself.
3. Very briefly, let each member of the group say what their idea is of 'the kingdom of God'. Then discuss the biblical idea of the kingdom.
4. Does the prayer 'Your will be done' frighten you? If it is done, do you think that you will be a better person and that this will be a better world?
5. Do you accept that God wants there to be justice in our world? If you do, what could you do about it? Read aloud Nehemiah's prayer and discuss how you, and your church, could take action for justice.
6. Spend some time thinking of places and situations in our world where the kingdom of God has not come and where the will of God is not done. Are you willing to pray for them 'Your kingdom come, Your will be done on earth as it is in heaven'?

Then have a time of silence.

Ask people to pray their own prayers aloud, if they want to.

Then perhaps use this meditation:

Meditation

Lord Jesus Christ, we remember that great prayer of yours in the Garden of Gethsemane:
'My Father, if it is not possible for this cup to be taken away, unless I drink it, may your will be done.'
Thank you that you prayed it.
Thank you that you did your Father's will.
Thank you that because you did we have the forgiveness of sins and eternal life.

Saviour of the world, help us to do the Father's will.
Show us where we aren't doing it.
Now, in a few minutes of silence, will you search our hearts?
Show us ourselves as you see us.
Show us those areas in our lives where we may need to pray that prayer . . .
'Father, not my will, but yours, be done' . . .
Saviour of the world, show us the blessedness of the Father's will . . .

Spend four or five minutes in silence, and bring it to an end by saying, 'Father, not my will, but yours be done . . .'

A Prayer for those who Suffer

> You are love
> and you see all the suffering,
> injustice, and misery,
> which reign in this world.
> Have pity, we implore you,
> on the work of your hands.
> Look mercifully on the poor,
> the oppressed, and all who are heavy laden
> with error, labour and sorrow.
> Fill our hearts with deep compassion for those who suffer,
> and hasten the coming of your kingdom of justice and truth.
> Eugene Bersier 1831–1889

Finally, say together: 'Our Father . . .'

10. Give Us This Day Our Daily Bread

Gavin has always remembered what a woman whom he met at a conference said about the Lord's Prayer – that Jesus put the prayer 'Give us this day our daily bread' before 'Forgive us our trespasses'. It's difficult to be too concerned about our sins if we are starving, so perhaps Jesus is telling us, by putting the petitions in that order, that our daily bread is just as much a matter of concern to God as the forgiveness of sins – even though our sins are of infinite importance and our starvation only of finite importance. But what we do about other people's starvation and hunger is of infinite importance – and we looked at it in chapter 6.

The Lord's Prayer is a model for all our praying, and it shows us that God knows what we need and is concerned that we have it. Our daily bread stands for all the things that we need – the basic material for keeping the human being going.

Some years ago Gavin met a man who had been teaching at a mission school in Ghana. Some of the children at the school were orphans and agonizingly poor. The man suddenly realized that, although he was teaching the children to pray to a heavenly

Father, 'Give us this day our daily bread', humanly speaking no one was giving it to them. Some of the children were malnourished, and the man knew that he had to do something about it.

It was the will of God that these children should have their daily bread. So, as someone who served God, he couldn't just teach them the words and leave it there. Prayerfully and penitently he set up a children's home – rather as George Müller had set up his orphanage in Bristol in the nineteenth century. And, as with George Müller, they would start the day with no food in the house, but somehow it would arrive on the doorstep. That man was a perfect example of someone being part of God's answer to their own prayers.

The letter of James is very blunt about people whose actions do not match their words.

What good is it, my brothers, if a man claims to have faith but has no deeds? Can such faith save him? Suppose a brother or sister is without clothes and daily food. If one of you says to him, 'Go, I wish you well: keep warm and well fed,' but does nothing about his physical needs, what good is it? In the same way, faith by itself, if it is not accompanied by action, is dead.

James 2:14–17 NIV

Bread for the body

It is possible to over-spiritualize the Bible. A few scholars suggest that what Jesus is telling us to pray for in this prayer is the daily bread of the Eucharist. But that is very unlikely to be right, since immediately after the Lord's Prayer in Luke's gospel, Jesus tells the story of a man going to ask his friend for three loaves of bread because an unexpected visitor has turned up.

One day Jesus was praying in a certain place. When he finished, one of his disciples said to him, 'Lord, teach us to pray, just as John taught his disciples.'
He said to them, 'When you pray, say:

> "Father,
> hallowed be your name,

Luke 11:1–13 NIV

89

your kingdom come.
Give us each day our daily bread.
Forgive us our sins,
    for we also forgive everyone who sins against us,
And lead us not into temptation." '

Then he said to them, 'Suppose one of you has a friend, and he goes to him at midnight and says, "Friend, lend me three loaves of bread, because a friend of mine on a journey has come to me, and I have nothing to set before him."

'Then the one inside answers, "Don't bother me. The door is already locked, and my children are with me in bed. I can't get up and give you anything." I tell you, though he will not get up and give him the bread because he is his friend, yet because of the man's persistence he will get up and give him as much as he needs.

'So I say to you: Ask and it will be given to you; seek and you will find; knock and the door will be opened to you. For everyone who asks receives; he who seeks finds; and to him who knocks, the door will be opened.

'Which of you fathers, if your son asks for a fish, will give him a snake instead? Or if he asks for an egg, will give him a scorpion? If you, then, who are evil, know how to give good gifts to your children, how much more will your Father in heaven give the Holy Spirit to those who ask him!'

Jesus was telling us to pray for the bread that we eat, and in this prayer he balances prayer for physical things with prayer for spiritual things. Our heavenly Father will never give us less than a human father would give us, and in Matthew's account of that story Jesus says, 'Which of you, if his son asks for bread, will give him a stone?' (Matthew 7:9).

Jesus was dealing with people who really knew what hunger was like. What shines out of the story of the feeding of the five thousand is his genuine anxiety that people were so malnourished that they would faint on the way home unless they got some more food.

Jesus never said that man does not live by eating bread. What he said, quoting the Old Testament, was 'Man does not live by bread *alone*.' The bread that is made from wheat or barley is to satisfy our human hunger. If we don't get enough of it we shall die from starvation – and millions of people are doing just that every year. They lose their physical lives because they don't have bread to eat.

But there is a bread which satisfies the hunger of the soul, and if we don't eat it then we lose our souls. It isn't that we die spiritually. It is that we don't really have any spiritual life: 'I tell you the truth, unless you can eat the flesh of the Son of Man and drink his blood, you have no life in you' (John 6:53 NIV).

Jesus is the bread of life, and he gives that bread to the world to eat by giving his life on the cross.

I am the bread of life. Your forefathers ate the manna in the desert, yet they died. But here is the bread that comes down from heaven, which a man may eat and not die. I am the living bread that came down from heaven. If anyone eats of this bread, he will live for ever. This bread is my flesh, which I will give for the life of the world. John 6:48–51 NIV

God is concerned for our material needs and our spiritual needs – for the whole person that he created. But the Lord's prayer does not say 'Give us this day our daily cake' – and even if they had had cakes in those days it would not have said it. Jesus is telling us to ask for our necessities.

Some of us may need a car, and if we do we can pray for one. It might be given to us. Christians have known this to happen, but it is unusual. What is more likely is that we shall discover how to manage our finances in order to get one. But it is unlikely (unfortunately!) to be a Porsche. That is a luxury, and although God has made a de luxe model world and not an economy model, that doesn't mean that a Christian lifestyle ought to be luxurious. There are too many starving people in the world for that.

John F. Kennedy once said that there is enough food in the world to feed all the people in the world – but what is lacking is the will to do it. It is the will of God that the hungry should be fed. But the will of God is often not done – and that is why we have to pray that it should be done and also be willing to do it ourselves.

It is a bizarre fact that one third of the world is too fat and that

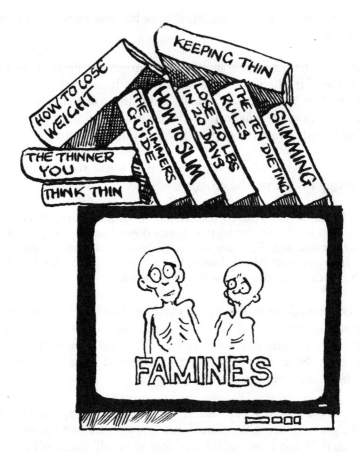

the other two thirds are too thin. We are on diets. They are desperate for the basic necessities of life. This is a serious matter, and we had better take it seriously. We shall be asked about it on the final day of judgement – and be delighted or appalled at what the risen Christ, who will be our judge, says to us.

Group Material for chapter 10:
GIVE US THIS DAY OUR DAILY BREAD

1. Read out Luke 11:1–13.
2. What do you think Jesus meant when he told his disciples to pray 'Give us this day our daily bread'? Do you pray for yours?

Or do you assume that the necessities of life will always be there automatically?

3. Discuss the points that have particularly struck you in the chapter and in the Bible readings.

4. Read out John 6:35–40.

5. Ask each person to say what they think it means, and also what it means to them.

Meditation and Prayers

Start with a time of silence.

Then ask people to pray out loud, if they would like to.

Then perhaps read out John 6:1–11 very slowly – with short silences between the sentences. People might like to shut their eyes and imagine they are there, or they might just listen in deep attention and ask God to speak to them through the words of scripture:

Some time after this, Jesus crossed to the far shore of the Sea of Galilee **John 6:1–11 NIV** (that is, the Sea of Tiberias), and a great crowd of people followed him because they saw the miraculous signs he had performed on the sick. Then Jesus went up on a mountainside and sat down with his disciples. The Jewish Passover Feast was near.

When Jesus looked up and saw a great crowd coming towards him, he said to Philip, 'Where shall we buy bread for these people to eat?' He asked this only to test him, for he already had in mind what he was going to do.

Philip answered him, 'Eight months' wages would not buy enough bread for each one to have a bite!'

Another of his disciples, Andrew, Simon Peter's brother, spoke up, 'Here is a boy with five small barley loaves and two small fish, but how far will they go among so many?'

Jesus said, 'Make the people sit down.' There was plenty of grass in that place, and the men sat down, about five thousand of them. Jesus then took the loaves, gave thanks, and distributed to those who were seated as much as they wanted. He did the same with the fish.

A Prayer for Each One of Us to Pray in our Heart

Lord Jesus, the needs of the world are very large – and when I think about them I feel helpless. So help me to remember that boy who gave his lunch to you — five little barley loaves and two little fish. Help me to remember what happened to them, in your hands. Help me to give what I can to you — to feed the world. Give us this day our daily bread.   Amen

Say together: 'Our Father . . .'

A Prayer from the Church of South India

O God our Father, by whose mercy and might the world turns safely into darkness and returns again to light. We give into your hands our unfinished tasks, our unsolved problems, and our unfulfilled hopes, knowing that only that which you bless will prosper. To your great love and protection we commit each other and all those we love, knowing that you alone are our sure defender, through Jesus Christ our Lord.   Amen

11. Forgive Us Our Sins

Sin isn't a very popular word these days. Some people say that to talk about sin is old-fashioned and unenlightened, and they don't like being made to feel guilty.

But sin is a fact of life. When we sin, what we are doing is to hurt someone or something – the environment, an animal, or a human being.

We hurt our environment when we pollute our seas and poison them with our waste and our effluents. The seas used to wash everything clean for us, but now we are putting such an evil mixture into them that in many places they can no longer do what God created them to do.

We sin against our environment when we cut down the world's great forests at the rate of thousands of living trees a day. The countries who cut them down desperately need the money. They are poor and getting poorer – while the selfish rich countries are getting richer.

One reason why the trees that give oxygen to the world are cut down is that some of us in the West would find our weekdays and our Sundays less enjoyable without our newspapers – millions of tons of paper that simply inform us of what happened yesterday and are out of date tomorrow.

We sin against an animal when we kill an elephant for its ivory tusks – and appalling though this is, we need to remember that elephants live in poor countries and not rich ones.

In the rich countries we keep animals as pets. In Britain we are especially attached to dogs, and the advertisers of a well known toilet tissue and a popular brand of paint know that we are. We smile delightedly as the Labrador puppy entangles itself in vast lengths of lavatory paper, and we are entranced with the Old English Sheepdog as it oversees the do-it-yourself decorating of its owner.

But we sin against our dogs and hurt them appallingly. The Yorkshire vet James Heriot, whose best-selling books have been serialized on television, told how one day he saw a little dog in the road, desperately running to try to catch up a car. The owners had simply thrown it out into the road because they wanted to be rid of it. Other dog owners do it too – sometimes on motorways.

James Heriot's story had a happy ending, because he rescued the dog and found it a happy home. But what about all the others? The usual ending of a dog's life when it is abandoned is to be put down by the RSPCA (who hate having to do it) and thrown on the enormous heap of unwanted, unloved creatures that no one wants to know about. When the RSPCA reproduced a photograph of one of those heaps on a poster and displayed it at Cruft's, the great British dog event of the year, people were deeply offended and demanded its removal.

We sin against a human being – and it could be ourself or someone else – when we sleep around and risk cervical cancer or AIDS, and when we fail to realize the emotional damage and hurt that promiscuity does to us.

We sin against human beings when we drive over the drink limit and risk the possibility that because of our action people may be crippled or killed.

Sin is a failure in love. Jesus said that the two great commandments are about loving God and our neighbour and ourself:

The first is, 'Hear, O Israel: The Lord our God, the Lord is one; and you shall love the Lord your God with all your heart, and with all your soul, and with all your mind, and with all your strength.' The second is this, 'You shall love your neighbour as yourself.' Mark 12:29–31 RSV

Only Jesus kept them

Jesus was the only person who has ever kept the commandments. Theologians speak about his 'sinlessness', which means that he never sinned. And that means that he never failed to love. When the Jews were trying to put him down he asked them, 'Can any of you prove me guilty of sin?' – and they couldn't. They accused him of it. They said he was possessed by a demon, and they said he was a glutton and drank too much. But they couldn't make the accusations stick. Even when it came to his trial they couldn't manage it:

The chief priests and the whole council sought false testimony against Jesus that they might put him to death, but they found none, though many false witnesses came forward. Matthew 26:59–60 RSV

It was only because of what Jesus finally said himself that they dared to crucify him. First of all he was silent. Then the high priest said to him:

'I adjure you by the living God, tell us if you are the Christ, the Son of God.' Jesus said to him, 'You have said so. But I tell you, hereafter you will see the Son of man seated at the right hand of Power, and coming on the clouds of heaven.' Then the high priest tore his robes, and said, 'He has uttered blasphemy. Why do we still need witnesses? You have now heard his blasphemy. What is your judgment?' They answered, 'He deserves death.' Verses 63–67

The Jews were not allowed to carry out the death sentence. The Romans who occupied their country had to do it for them. And as the Roman soldiers nailed Jesus to the cross Jesus prayed for them: 'Father forgive them; for they know not what they do' (Luke 23:34 RSV).

What happens to our sin?

So what happens when God forgives us or when we forgive another person? Where does the sin go to – the sinner's failure to love that results in a person or an animal or the earth being damaged or hurt? The pain is in the creature who has been sinned against. If someone beats you up, it is you who will be hurt. So you could say (and probably would!) that whoever did it had sinned against you.

But after all the tragic and terrible sins that King David committed he cried out to God, 'Against thee, thee only have I sinned' (Psalm 51:4). He had committed adultery with Bathsheba – which damaged him as well as her. He had had her husband Uriah murdered by getting him sent to the thick of the battle. But because God created the whole universe and all the creatures in it (and holds it all in existence through his word of power) all sins are ultimately committed against God.

So God takes action to deal with them. The Christian faith is that he did it through Jesus Christ, and when Paul is explaining this to the church in Corinth he writes that 'in Christ God was reconciling the world to himself, not counting their trespasses against them . . .' (2 Corinthians 5:19 RSV).

But people sometimes say 'Why can't God just forgive people's sins and then forget about them? Why make such a fuss about it? And why did Christ have to die for us, and what did it do anyway?'

The answer is that sin spoils things. It spoils us and it spoils our relationships – with God and with other people. A sin does something. And what it does doesn't just go away. It stays around – until it is really taken away.

The forgiveness of our sins

When I became a Christian the curate whom I mentioned earlier in this book, John Collins, did something that helped me to understand. He asked me if I had ever sinned, and since there wasn't much doubt about that we went on from there. He held out his hands with their palms upwards. His left hand represented me and his right hand represented Jesus on the cross. On the hand that was me he put a book to represent my sin, and then said some words from Isaiah: 'All we like sheep have gone astray: we have turned every one to his own way; and the Lord has laid on him the iniquity of us all' (Isaiah 53:6 RSV).

As John said those last words he moved the book from his left hand on to his right hand. Then he asked me where my sin was. A child could have told him. It was on Jesus. All I had to do was to believe it.

John Bunyan tells the same story in the marvellous words of *Pilgrim's Progress*:

Now I saw in my Dream that the highway up which Christian was to go was fenced on either side with a Wall, and that Wall is called Salvation. Up this way therefore did burdened Christian run, but not without great difficulty, because of the load on his back.

He ran thus till he came to a place somewhat ascending; and upon that place stood a Cross, and a little below in the bottom, a Sepulchre. So I saw in my Dream, that just as Christian came up with the Cross, his Burden loosed from off his shoulders, and fell from off his back, and began to tumble, and so continued to do, till it came to the mouth of the Sepulchre, where it fell in, and I saw it no more.

Then was Christian glad and lightsome, and said with a merry heart, 'He hath given me rest by his sorrow, and life by his death.' Then he stood still awhile to look and wonder; for it was very surprising to him, that the sight of the Cross should thus ease him of his Burden. He looked therefore, and looked again, even till the springs that were in his head sent the waters down his cheeks. Now as he stood looking and weeping, behold three Shining Ones came to him and saluted him with 'Peace be to Thee.' So the first said to him, 'Thy sins be forgiven thee'; the second stript him of his Rags, and clothed him with change of Raiment; the third also set a mark on his forehead, and gave him a Roll with a Seal upon it, which he bade him look on as he ran, and that he should give it in at the Celestial Gate. So they went on their way. Then Christian gave three leaps for joy, and went on, singing,

Thus far did I come laden with my sin;
Nor could aught ease the grief that I was in
Till I came hither: What a place is this!
Must here be the beginning of my bliss?
Must here the Burden fall from off my back?
Must here the strings that bound it to me crack?
Blest Cross! blest Sepulchre! blest rather be
The Man that there was put to shame for me.

All Christians do not have the same experience as John Bunyan. They cannot remember a particular day when they realized that Christ died for them. But they know that he did, and it is the shortest Christian creed we can ever say – and all we ever need to say: 'Christ died for me!'

Once we get that straight we shall never get confused about the petition in the Lord's Prayer which this chapter is about.

As we forgive . . .

The disciples had asked Jesus to teach them to pray, and this is the prayer he taught them. 'This is how you should pray . . .' and that means how all disciples should pray. Only disciples can pray the Lord's Prayer, and only disciples can understand it.

Sometimes people who don't understand and who aren't disciples tear the phrase 'Forgive us our sins as we forgive those who sin against us' out of the prayer and say that before we can be forgiven we have to forgive. But it is only when we have been forgiven that we can forgive. Then we shall be able to do it up to seventy-seven times – and by then we shall have lost count!

Matthew 18:21–35 NIV Peter came to Jesus and asked, 'Lord, how many times shall I forgive my brother when he sins against me? Up to seven times?'

Jesus answered, 'I tell you, not seven times, but seventy-seven times.

'Therefore, the kingdom of heaven is like a king who wanted to settle accounts with his servants. As he began the settlement, a man who owed him ten thousand talents was brought to him. Since he was not able to pay, the master ordered that he and his wife and his children and all that he had be sold to repay the debt.

'The servant fell on his knees before him. "Be patient with me," he begged, "and I will pay back everything." The servant's master took pity on him, cancelled the debt and let him go.

'But when that servant went out, he found one of his fellow-servants who owed him a hundred denarii. He grabbed him and began to choke him. "Pay back what you owe me!" he demanded.

'His fellow-servant fell to his knees and begged, "Be patient with me, and I will pay you back."

'But he refused. Instead, he went off and had the man thrown into prison until he could pay the debt. When the other servants saw what had happened, they were greatly distressed and went and told their master everything that had happened.

'Then the master called the servant in. "You wicked servant," he said, "I cancelled all that debt of yours because you begged me to. Shouldn't you have had mercy on your fellow-servant just as I had on you?" In anger his master turned him over to the jailers to be tortured until he should pay back all he owed.

'This is how my heavenly Father will treat each of you unless you forgive your brother from your heart.'

Forgiveness is about accepting the hurt that someone has done to us, bearing the pain of it (and we can only do it through Christ), and still loving the person who hurt us.

Forgiveness breaks the chain of causality because he who 'forgives' you – out of love – takes upon himself the consequences of what *you* have done. Forgiveness, therefore, always entails a sacrifice. The price you must pay for your own liberation through another's sacrifice, is that you in turn must be willing to liberate in the same way, irrespective of the consequences to yourself.

Dag Hammarskjöld, *Markings*

In *The Hiding Place* Corrie ten Boom tells how her former jailer came up to her after a church service where she had spoken. He had stood guard over her and her sister Betsy as they were processed in the shower room at the terrible Ravensbruck camp. Now he came up to her, smiling and bowing. 'How grateful I am for your message, Fräulein,' he said. 'To think that, as you say, he has washed my sins away!' He held out his hand to her, but she couldn't take it.

I, who had preached so often to the people in Bloemendaal the need to forgive, kept my hand at my side.

Even as the angry, vengeful thoughts boiled through me, I saw the sin of them. Jesus Christ had died for this man; was I going to ask for more? 'Lord Jesus,' I prayed, 'forgive me and help me to forgive him.'

101

I tried to smile, I struggled to raise my hand, I could not. I felt nothing, not the slightest spark of warmth or charity. And so again I breathed a silent prayer: 'Jesus, I cannot forgive him. Give me Your forgiveness.'

As I took his hand the most incredible thing happened. From my shoulder along my arm and through my hand a current seemed to pass from me to him, while into my heart sprang a love for this stranger that almost overwhelmed me.

And so I discovered that it is not on our forgiveness any more than on our goodness that the world's healing hinges, but on His. When He tells us to love our enemies, He gives, along with the command, the love itself.

Group material, prayers and meditation for chapter 11:
FORGIVE US OUR SINS

1. Start with a short time of silence. Then say the Lord's Prayer together.
2. Read out the Bible passage from Matthew 18:21–35.
3. Ask each person to think of a situation in their own life when it has been (or is still) hard to forgive. Then discuss what it is that makes it so difficult. Was it that they were hurt themselves, or was it someone they loved who was hurt?
4. Read out the extract from *Pilgrim's Progress*, and ask each person as they listen to reflect on it whether they know that they themselves are forgiven sinners. Ask people to share with each other what they thought when they listened.
5. Read out the following extract, from a marvellous book by Sister Margaret Magdalen called *Jesus – Man of Prayer*.

God takes this matter of praying for forgiveness very seriously. The capacity to pray in this way is what makes us priests, following the footsteps of our great high priest pleading for mercy for those who need it.

In Isaiah 59:1–16 we are given a picture of a society which could easily be our own. It speaks of 'hands defiled with blood', lips that 'have spoken lies', tongues that have muttered wickedness. No one goes to law honestly, 'their feet run to evil,' 'they make haste to shed innocent blood', 'destruction and desolation are in their highways', 'the way of peace they know not', 'there is no justice' but 'oppression and revolt', 'truth has fallen in the public squares and uprightness cannot enter', etc.

And we are told, 'The Lord saw it, and it displeased him . . . He saw that there was no man, and wondered that there was no one to intercede.'

He was amazed that no one had been sufficiently concerned to stand before him as priest and intercessor and plead mercy for these benighted people heading for their own destruction.

He invites us to participte with him in this priestly work by praying 'Father, forgive them', not simply because of our own injured feelings and battered pride, but on behalf of those who flagrantly defy God's laws and have no intention of asking for forgiveness. We are called to stand on the Godward side of the evildoers.

When we see on our TV screens the artist's impression of a man wanted for abducting a child or shooting the cashier in a sub post office, what emotions are stirred? A desire for revenge? Waves of sympathy for the relatives? A sick feeling at the increasing violence in our society? A longing for justice and humankindness? Maybe a mixture of them all? But do we pray 'Father, forgive him', opening up a channel for God's redemptive power to reach him? Does it make *us* turn to God in penitence and confession for all the seeds of that same violence which lurk in our own hearts – oh yes, carefully held in check by our social upbringing, conditioning and, maybe, religious training, but nevertheless *there*? It should. There is a purity needed for the work of intercession. Nowhere is this more clearly expressed than in the Lord's promise to Solomon after the dedication of the temple as the house consecrated to the praise of his glory. He said, 'If my people, who are called by my name, humble themselves and pray and seek my face and turn from their wicked ways, then I will hear from heaven and will forgive their sin and heal their land' (2 Chronicles 7:14).

6. Discuss the above passage.

What are the sins and situations in our world that make you most angry? Are you willing to pray for the people involved?

7. Read out the extract from *The Hiding Place*. Then have a time of silence followed by a time of open prayer.

Finish as you started, by saying the Lord's Prayer together.

12. Lead Us Not Into Temptation

A long time ago John Stott told a story about a small boy who was going out to play in the wood behind his house. As he was getting his things together his mother called out to say that when he got there he wasn't to go swimming. 'No, I won't,' said the small boy. 'I promise.'

He got on with his preparations and his mother got on with his lunch. But when she went to put his lunch box in his bag she was annoyed and upset to find his swimming trunks neatly packed in.

'But Johnnie, you *promised*!' she said reproachfully. 'So what are these doing in here?' 'Yes,' said Johnnie. 'I know I promised. But I put them in just in case I was tempted.'

It isn't God who tempts us

James 1:13 (NIV) says, 'When tempted, no one should say, "God is tempting me." For God cannot be tempted by evil, nor does he tempt anyone.' But we are told that immediately after Jesus' baptism, 'Jesus was led by the Spirit into the desert to be tempted by the devil' (Matthew 4:1 NIV). The devil does the tempting, but it was God who led Jesus into the place where he would be tempted. So what about us? And if that happened to Jesus, why does he seem to be telling us to pray that the same thing won't happen to us?

The answer is that we make 'Lead us not into temptation' into a prayer all on its own. But it belongs within the whole of the Lord's Prayer, and especially with 'Deliver us from evil' which comes immediately afterwards.

There was a distinctive way that the ancient Hebrews said things (technically called 'Hebrew parallelism') and we can see it in the Psalms. First they say what they want to in one way, and then they say it again immediately in another way. Look at the first verse of Psalm 37 (NJB):

> Do not get heated about the wicked
> or envy those who do wrong.
> Quick as the grass they wither,
> fading like the green of the fields.

and verse 8:

> Refrain from anger,
> leave rage aside.

They add a second phrase or description to the first one. It isn't a new idea, but the same one seen from a new angle. And it seems very important to go on from praying 'Lead us not into temptation' into 'Deliver us from evil'. When we pray that, we admit that we are terribly vulnerable. If we are to be led into a situation where we shall be tempted and tested, then we admit now – before it ever happens – that without the mighty help of God we shall be overcome by evil. So we cry out now for deliverance then.

Matthew 4:1–11
NIV

Then Jesus was led by the Spirit into the desert to be tempted by the devil. After fasting for forty days and forty nights, he was hungry. The tempter came to him and said, 'If you are the Son of God, tell these stones to become bread.'

Jesus answered, 'It is written, "Man does not live on bread alone, but on every word that comes from the mouth of God."'

Then the devil took him to the holy city and had him stand on the highest point of the temple. 'If you are the Son of God,' he said, 'throw yourself down. For it is written:

> "He will command his angels concerning you,
> and they will lift you up in their hands,
> so that you will not strike your foot against a stone."'

Jesus answered him, 'It is also written, "Do not put the Lord your God to the test."'

Again, the devil took him to a very high mountain and showed him all the kingdoms of the world and their splendour. 'All this I will give you,' he said, 'if you will bow down and worship me.'

Jesus said to him, 'Away from me, Satan! For it is written: "Worship the Lord your God, and serve him only." '

Then the devil left him, and angels came and attended him.

'Lead us not into temptation' is saying to God, 'We really don't trust ourselves to cope with life – and if you allow us to be tempted we shall cave in – unless you help us.'

Watch and pray!

When Jesus faced the greatest test of his life he prayed beforehand, in the terrible agony of the Garden of Gethsemane:

'My Father, if it be possible, let this cup pass from me; nevertheless, not as I will, but as thou wilt.' And he came to the disciples and found them sleeping; and he said to Peter, 'So, could you not watch with me one hour? Watch and pray that you may not enter into temptation; the spirit indeed is willing, but the flesh is weak.' Again, for the second time, he went away and prayed, 'My Father, if this cannot pass unless I drink it, thy will be done.' And again he came and found them sleeping, for their eyes were heavy.

Matthew 26:39–43 RSV

Jesus prayed beforehand. Peter and James and John didn't. We know the result in both cases. The glory of God shining out in the death and resurrection of Christ on the one hand – and the desolation and disgrace of Peter's denial on the other.

A friend of mine has been having a great struggle with a particular temptation recently, and in the midst of it she came across this poem by Amy Carmichael in a book called *Edges of His Ways*:

> Before the winds that blow do cease,
> Teach me to dwell within Thy calm;
> Before the pain has passed in peace,
> Give me, my God, to sing a psalm.
> Let me not lose the chance to prove
> The fullness of enabling love.
> O love of God, do this for me:
> Maintain a constant victory.

Before I leave the desert land
For meadows of immortal flowers,
Lead me where streams at thy command
Flow by the borders of the hours,
That when the thirsty come, I may
Show them the fountains in the way.
O love of God, do this for me:
Maintain a constant victory.

The strange and difficult thing is that we need to be tested and tempted. Otherwise we never develop a strong faith – and we do that as we use and exercise what little, weak faith we already have; rather like doing spiritual exercises to develop our spiritual muscles. We can do that when we are going through the most difficult patches of our lives.

James 1:2–15
NIV

Consider it pure joy, my brothers, whenever you face trials of many kinds, because you know that the testing of your faith develops perseverance. Perseverance must finish its work so that you may be mature and complete, not lacking anything. If any of you lacks wisdom, he should ask God, who gives generously to all without finding fault, and it will be given to him. But when he asks, he must believe and not doubt, because he who doubts is like a wave of the sea, blown and tossed by the wind. That man should not think he will receive anything from the Lord; he is a double-minded man, unstable in all he does.

The brother in humble circumstances ought to take pride in his high position. But the one who is rich should take pride in his low position, because he will pass away like a wild flower. For the sun rises with scorching heat and withers the plant; its blossom falls and its beauty is destroyed. In the same say, the rich man will fade away even while he goes about his business.

Blessed is the man who perseveres under trial, because when he has stood the test, he will receive the crown of life that God has promised to those who love him.

When tempted, no one should say, 'God is tempting me.' For God cannot be tempted by evil, nor does he tempt anyone; but each one is tempted when, by his own evil desire, he is dragged away and enticed. Then, after desire has conceived, it gives birth to sin; and sin when it is full-grown, gives birth to death.

The testing of our faith

Back in the Old Testament Moses tells the people of Israel why God led them in the wilderness in the way that he did:

108

You shall remember all the way which the Lord your God has led you Deuteronomy 8:2–3 RSV these forty years in the wilderness, that he might humble you, testing you to know what was in your heart, whether you would keep his commandments, or not. And he humbled you and let you hunger and fed you with manna, which you did not know, nor did your fathers know; that he might make you know that man does not live by bread alone, but that man lives by everything that proceeds out of the mouth of the Lord.

It was with an appeal to this verse from Deuteronomy that Jesus fought off the evil one when he was tempted. He was physically hungry. But the will of God mattered more than his physical appetite. In John's gospel, when he has been talking with the woman by the well in Samaria, his disciples come along with the food they have been to buy and urge him to eat it. But he says to them, 'I have food to eat of which you do not know . . . My food is to do the will of him who sent me, and to accomplish his work' (John 4:32–33 RSV).

We shall often be tempted to satisfy our physical hungers in ways that God doesn't want us to. One of the hungers that we shall be tempted about is our sexual hunger, and the temptation can come to us through television and newspapers, books and advertisements, and the general attitude of the world around us to sexual 'freedom'.

In *Something More* Catherine Marshall tells a true story that was first published in *Guideposts* magazine. A woman whom Catherine Marshall calls Mary was married to Bill, a travelling salesman, and they had three children, the youngest a baby girl. The couple went to church and were active there, and they had both become friends with an attractive man called John Ames.

When Bill was away John would run Mary and the children to church, and she suddenly realized that she was becoming attracted to him. She knew she had to resist the temptation, so the next Sunday she took the children very early to Sunday school in order to avoid him. But the following Sunday he came even earlier and gave them all a lift. The attraction was intensifying and it was electric. Then, writes Catherine Marshall,

One night Mary forced herself to face the issue. 'I made myself think through the end results if John and I kept on the road we were going. A romantic interlude, nothing more? To think so would be kidding myself. Rather, probably a broken home. My husband's life cruelly hurt and twisted. Worse still for our children. And tawdriness as my reward. On the other side was the frightening intensity of the electricity between John and me.

'In desperation, I dropped on my knees. "Oh God! This is too much for me." It was a cry wrung out of me. "I can't fight any more. I turn this battle over to You." That night I slept calmly.'

The next day, with her husband still out of town, Mary spent the entire day cleaning – closets, drawers, cupboards, windows. In some way, it must have been symbolic.

That evening, after the children were in bed, John Ames appeared at the front door. 'Bill's not home', Mary told him. But he came in anyway.

Mary didn't ask her caller to sit down. She remained standing in the centre of the room bathed in a cone of light from the electrical fixture overhead. There was an awkward interlude during which John Ames made persistent small talk, his eyes fastened on Mary. As she concentrated on Jesus as represented by that light, she felt herself becoming less aware of John and more and more aware of the enveloping light of God all around her.

Finally her caller noticed the baby asleep on the sofa. 'Don't you want me to carry her to her crib?' he asked.

Mary nodded, but did not follow John into the darkness of the adjoining bedroom. Somehow she knew that she must not. There in the darkness John's arms would reach for her as inevitably as – No, *she must stay in the light*. As long as she stood in the light, the values she really cared about – her marriage, the home she and Bill had made together, their children – would be safe.

John remained in the bedroom for what seemed like an eternity, waiting for her, Mary thought. At last he emerged. For a long moment he stood looking at Mary, indecision written on his face. At last, reluctantly, he left.

'Then I understood,' the author wrote, 'the truth of the scripture teaching that there's nothing wrong with being tempted. It's what we *do* with the temptation that matters.'

Group material, prayers and meditation for chapter 12:
LEAD US NOT INTO TEMPTATION

1. Read aloud James 1:2–15.
2. Discuss the passage and a few points that have specially struck you in this chapter.

3. What do you think it means to pray 'Lead us not into temptation; but deliver us from evil'?
4. Read aloud Matthew 4:1–11.
5. Discuss the three areas of Jesus' temptation and see how they apply to us: bread, magical powers, and the worship of a false god.
6. When Jesus faced temptation he prayed. When Peter faced temptation he didn't. What can we learn from that – and how can we apply it to our own lives? Can we know beforehand that we are going to be tempted? Discuss Catherine Marshall's story about Mary. And think about the small boy and his swimming trunks.

Prayers and Meditation

[Note to leader: leave quite long silences between each part of the prayer, so that people can meditate and reflect on it as well as pray it]

Let us be quiet now in the presence of God . . .
Our Father . . . lead us not into temptation . . . but deliver us from evil . . .
In the silence of our hearts, let us ask Christ to show us our hearts . . .
'Behold, thou desirest truth in the inward being; therefore teach me wisdom in my secret heart . . .' (Psalm 51:6 RSV).
Show us where we are weak, Lord God . . . Help us to be honest with you about our temptations . . . our desires . . . our longings . . .
Show us what's right and what's wrong . . .
Thank you that the testing of our faith develops perseverance . . . we can see that that is true . . . so help us to consider it pure joy when we face trials and testings . . .
Help us to persevere . . . so that we may be mature and complete, not lacking anything.
You know the situation of each one of us . . . and you know our problems and our difficulties . . .
You have promised that if we lack wisdom and ask you for it, then you will give it to us . . .
So we ask now . . . for wisdom to know what to do in our temptations and in our trials and in our testing . . .

111

Let us be silent now, in the presence of God . . . and we shall bring the silence to an end with a prayer . . .
[*Note to leader: time the silence! Not less than three minutes – not more than five.*]

A Prayer of John Baillie

> Teach me, O God, so to use all the circumstances of my life today that they may bring forth in me the fruits of holiness rather than the fruits of sin.
> Let me use disappointments as material for patience . . .
> Let me use success as material for thankfulness . . .
> Let me use suspense as material for perseverance . . .
> Let me use danger as material for courage . . .
> Let me use reproach as material for longsuffering . . .
> Let me use praise as material for humility . . .
> Let me use pleasure as material for temperance . . .
> Let me use pains as material for endurance . . .   Amen

Suggest that people pray their own prayers out loud.

Then pray the Lord's Prayer together.

Final Prayers

> Shine, Jesus, shine
> Fill this land with the Father's glory;
> Blaze, Spirit, blaze,
> Set our hearts on fire.
> Flow, river, flow,
> Flood the nations with grace and mercy;
> Send forth Your word, Lord,
> And let there be light.

Lord Jesus Christ, Light of the World, send us out now in the power of your Holy Spirit to shine as a light in the world to the glory of God the Father.   Amen

Sources of Quoted Material

INTRODUCTION

The song 'Shine, Jesus, Shine' by Graham Kendrick is Copyright 1988 Make Way Music, published by Kingsway Publications and is used by permission of the publishers.

CHAPTER 1

C. H. Dodd, *The Founder of Christianity*, Collins 1979, p. 72.

CHAPTER 2

C. S. Lewis, *The Magician's Nephew*, Penguin 1959.

CHAPTER 3

Charles Williams, *The Descent of the Dove: An Account of the Holy Spirit in the Church*, Paternoster Press 1939.
William Barclay, Daily Study Bible, *The Gospel of John*, Saint Andrew Press 1955, vol. 2, p. 194.
William Barclay, Daily Study Bible, *Romans*, Saint Andrew Press 1955, p. 105.
The Collect for Pentecost, *The Book of Common Prayer*, Crown copyright, used by permission of Eyre and Spottiswoode.

CHAPTER 4

William Temple, *Citizen and Churchman*, Eyre and Spottiswoode 1941, p. 98.
Christopher Bryan, *Nightfall*, Lion Publishing 1986.
Song from *The Muppet Movie*, Copyright © 1979 Henson Associates Inc.
John Robinson, *In the End, God*, Collins/Fontana 1968. Used by permission of the publishers.

Helder Camara, 'King's Son', Copyright © H. Camara from V. Zundel (Ed.), *The Lion Book of Famous Prayers*, Lion Publishing 1983.

CHAPTER 5

'Draw near with faith . . .' and 'We are the Body of Christ . . .', *The Alternative Service Book 1980*, The Order for Holy Communion Rite A, Copyright © The Central Board of Finance of the Church of England 1980. Used by permission.
Caroline Collier, *The 20th-Century Plague: What will happen if we can't stop AIDS?* Copyright © Christian Medical Fellowship, Lion Publishing 1987.
John Stott, *Christian Counter-Culture*, IVP 1978.
Alan Paton prayer, taken from *Instrument of Thy Peace*, new edition Ulverscroft 1986.

CHAPTER 6

Ernest Becker, *The Denial of Death*, Collier-Macmillan 1973.
William Barclay, Daily Study Bible, *Romans*, p. 54.
C. S. Lewis, *The Last Battle*, Penguin 1964.

CHAPTER 7

Frank Lake, *Clinical Theology*, Darton, Longman and Todd 1966.

CHAPTER 8

A. F. Knight and Fridemann W. Golka, *The Song of Songs and Jonah: Revelation of God*, The Handsel Press, Edinburgh 1988.
George Appleton, 'O God, I thank thee for all the creatures . . .', taken from the *Oxford Book of Prayer*, OUP 1985.

CHAPTER 10

Prayer from the Church of South India, from prayers for the Decade of Evangelism, distributed by the Anglican Consultative Council.

CHAPTER 11

Dag Hammarskjöld, *Markings*, Faber and Faber 1964. Used by permission.

Corrie ten Boom. *The Hiding Place*, Hodder and Stoughton and Christian Literature Crusade 1971, p. 220.

Sister Margaret Magdalen, CSMV, *Jesus – Man of Prayer*, Hodder and Stoughton 1987. Used by permission of the publishers.

CHAPTER 12

Amy Carmichael, 'Before the winds that blow . . .', *Edges of His Ways*, SPCK 1955.

Catherine Marshall, *Something More*, Hodder and Stoughton 1974. Used by permission of the publishers.

Bible versions marked:

NIV   are from the New International Version Copyright © 1973, 1978 by the International Bible Society

RSV   are from the Revised Standard Version Copyright © 1952, 1971 by the Division of Christian Education of the National Council of Churches of Christ in the United States of America

NJB   are from the New Jerusalem Bible Copyright © 1985 by Darton, Longman and Todd Ltd and Doubleday and Company.

GNB   are from the Good News Bible 4th edition, Copyright © 1976 by the American Bible Society

NEB   are from the New English Bible Copyright © 1970 Oxford University Press and Cambridge University Press.

THANK GOD FOR THAT!
by Tim Mayfield and James Jones
with illustrations by Taffy

In response to many requests . . . an adult equivalent of *Following Jesus* (written by James Jones).

For enquirers and adults considering church membership, here are 31 readings which provide practical steps towards Christian faith. Each short section considers a different aspect of what it means to commit oneself to God, and contains a Bible passage (printed out in full), thoughtful comments and a prayer.

Based on an effective scheme of parish evangelism and training, *Thank God For That* will be welcomed by parishes and church centres, house groups and individuals.

Tim Mayfield is director of evangelism in a Halifax parish. James Jones is Vicar of Emmanuel, South Croydon; now well-known as an author and broadcaster, he specialized in family services when at Christ Church, Clifton. His books include a series of three for BRF aimed at young people (*Following Jesus; Serving Jesus; Praying With Jesus*). Taffy's work is familiar from cartoon, filmstrip and video.

'I am very happy to endorse the book, for I find it a most useful resource which could be given to people finding their way into faith.'

Canon John Finney
(Officer for the Decade of Evangelism)